Neue Gedichte
New Poems

Neue Gedichte/New Poems

RAINER MARIA RILKE

Translated by Stephen Cohn

CARCANET

First published in Great Britain in 1992 by
Carcanet Press Limited
4th Floor, Conavon Court
12–16 Blackfriars Street
Manchester M3 5BQ

Revised paperback edition 1997

The German text of the *Neue Gedichte* is published by Insel
Verlag, Frankfurt am Main. First published: *Neue Gedichte*, 1907;
Der Neuen Gedichte anderer Teil, 1908.

A CIP catalogue record for this book
is available from the British Library.
ISBN 1 85754 323 8

The publisher acknowledges financial assistance from the
Arts Council of England.

Printed and bound in England by SRP Ltd, Exeter

Contents

5

Acknowledgements

I would like to thank Ray Ockenden of Wadham College and Peter Porter who have both, and for a second time, given me their generous help in these translations of Rilke's poetry. I wish to dedicate two of my translations from Part Two of the *Neue Gedichte*: 'Black Cat' is for Peter Porter, and 'The Sundial' is for Sylvia Platt.

Two books have been especially useful to me: J.B. Leishman's *Rainer Maria Rilke, New Poems* (Hogarth Press, 1964), and the *Rilke Kommentar* by August Stahl (Winkler Verlag, 1978).

S.C.

Introduction

> ...Rilke, whom *die Dinge* bless:
> The Santa Claus of loneliness.

So W.H. Auden writes in the *New Year Letter*. Auden deeply admired Rilke as a poet, all the more perhaps because he himself believed that a poet, like other men, must live as a social being, undertaking the duties of ordinary men and sharing their common joys and sorrows. That might be said to be an article and tradition of English romantic belief.

> Farewell, farewell, the heart that lives alone,
> Housed in a dream, at distance from the kind!

So Wordsworth had written. But no one could say that Rilke's heart lived *alone*. He was indeed a Santa Claus, bringing to himself and to his readers the wonderfully and meticulously tentative feeling for things, the exploration of things, of which his poetry has the secret. And never more so than in the two parts of the *Neue Gedichte*, the poems in which Rilke's peculiar genius first unmistakably showed itself.

His own kind of solitude was, indeed, the condition for the creation of Rilke's art. Out of that solitary condition he brings us a unique social and shared offering. In a very special sense he seems to live with us as sentient and sensitive human beings in his own kind of intimacy, as if 'the things' blessed us as well as him. The inwardness, the belonging-togetherness of this (in German the *Zusammengehörigkeitsgefühl*) has a special quality which irritates some readers and perhaps particularly irritates other and different kinds of poet. 'Rilke was a *jerk*', wrote John Berryman in one of his *Dream Songs*. All this really means is that the tone of Rilke's gentle, questing intimacy is quite different from that much less easy, much more self-conscious one trailed before us by the fiercely competitive American poet. All poets can do harm to their fellow men and women in their own way; although Berryman subscribed as conscientiously as Auden, or as Wordsworth himself, to the doctrine of our needs and duties – 'the human heart by which we live' – he created social and marital havoc on a scale which makes Rilke's with-drawal from the usual demands of love and marriage seem – as indeed it was – a scrupulous necessity for his survival as a poet, a way of exercising his own sort of moral humanity. Rilke remained deeply attached to his wife and daughter, in spite of the fact that he could not and did not live with them, and was always anxious for their welfare.

His solicitude towards his daughter at the time of her wedding is one of the most touching episodes in his life and letters.

But this is all by the way. A poet's biography is of course important for his poetry, for our response to and understanding of it, but it may hardly impinge on the nature of the poetry itself, and this is especially true in Rilke's case. His poetry could indeed be said to be about scenes and episodes from common life, but not in the same way that Wordsworth made that claim on behalf of the *Lyrical Ballads*. Common life for Rilke is a more inward and more subtle affair, but every bit as absorbing, and giving as much enjoyment as food for thought. In the *Neue Gedichte* we feel again and again that some quite well-known scene, story or piece of nature has been so entered into by the poet that it has delivered up to him, in words at once exact and hesitant, the inmost form and meaning of itself. Rilke is one of those rare poets who seem not so much to create as to reveal. If Auden is right that 'the things' bless him, it is because he has given a voice to the hitherto dumb mystery of their secret being.

This is the case with such a well-known poem as 'Das Karussell' – 'The Merry-Go-Round'. At first reading it might strike one as charming, certainly, but fairly obvious: the description of the fair, the children, the painted animals on which they ride, the circular motion with which comes back in turn the white elephant, the growling red lion, the lifelike stag with the little girl in blue on his back. But the still centre of the poem, as it were, gradually emerges from this brilliant verbal charade. It lies in the incongruity of passing existence as the merry-go-round reveals it. It is because neither animals nor children seem real, in this breathless masque of jollity, that we can have sudden glimpses of the true nature of both, glimpses mingled with and almost indistinguishable from the confused repetitive force and blindness of living. The living creatures, the little girl in blue, the little boy in white who rides the lion and holds on with his small hot hands 'dieweil der Löwe Zähne zeigt und Zunge' – while the dreadful beast displays its teeth and its tongue – have the ecstasy and pathos of life caught in its unending mechanical round of activity and not realising it: the very young ones are solemnly absorbed in the business; the older girls, still enjoying the childish sport, are suspended between such enjoyment and the sharper absorptions of puberty – literally suspended, for they gaze around everywhere as they ride, looking both for admiration and for possible admirers.

> A small white elephant goes sailing by,
> the lion bears a little boy in white,
> the fearsome creature shows its teeth and glares,
> the hot excited hands hold very tight.

And so they ride and so they circle round
and round again, and lively girls are there
for whom such games are practically outgrown
whose eyes look everywhere, search everywhere.

Rilke has an extraordinary sensitivity towards such moments of suspension and division in the young, as he has for all living things in the toils of the mechanical, like the panther in the zoo of the Jardin des Plantes.

Many of the more complex and subtle poems of the *Neue Gedichte* come in the second part, poems such as 'Leda', 'Death of the Beloved', 'Samuel Appears before Saul', 'Gold', 'The Group' (a poem inspired by Picasso's famous picture *Les Saltimbanques*). One of the most beautiful and fluid is 'Leda', a poem very well worth comparing with Yeats's poem 'Leda and the Swan'. Unlike Yeats, who is absorbed by the mythological implications of the subject, Rilke fastens on what might be termed its 'form', in the Platonic sense, the wonder of an actual event – as it were both social and biological – and how it could have come about. Rilke knows that the girl was betrayed but not deceived: she realised at once what was going on, a perception that echoes through the whole shadowy world of sexual innocence and knowledge.

> ...she seeing him draw near
> within the swan soon recognised the God
> and could not fail to see what he desired.
> Yet the deception had secured the deed...

Jupiter has not just made use of the swan: he finds himself becoming it in the act of love.

> Locked in her lap and every inch a swan
> he felt a feather grow on every feather.

As a result of his interest in Russia and in Russian poetry, in which he was encouraged by his mistress Lou Andreas-Salomé, herself a fluent Russian speaker, Rilke actually wrote a few poems in Russian, which she described as being 'quite ungrammatical but strangely effective'. It is not without interest to compare his poem 'A Prophet' with Pushkin's marvellous 'Prorok', an electrifying poem with the same title which Dostoevsky used to read aloud to his friends in high thrilling tones. Once again, Rilke's interest is concentrated on some innerness in the subject, in this case the prophet's relation to his and our image of God. Not so dissimilar is the haunting longer poem from the first part of the *Neue Gedichte*, 'Orpheus. Eurydike. Hermes', in which Rilke explores what the dead might feel like in *being* dead. Orpheus has been promised that Eurydice can come back to him from Hades and follow him to the upper world, provided he never looks back during their journey. Of course he does, and Hermes, her escort, has to lead her back to the nether world. But being dead she has no idea what is happening; and when the gods' messenger, with pity in his voice, tells her that her husband has looked back, 'she did not understand him, murmured: *Who?*' With patient, uncertain steps Eurydice turns to go back 'along that strip of pathway over meadows', without knowing why she was there, and who the figure was who yearned after her, 'unrecognisable and indistinct'.

These versions in English invent a language, the language of 'Rilke-in-English', in something of the same way that Rilke himself had reinvented in German the pure and pellucid language of the great Romantic poet Hölderlin. They are also sensitive to the poems in the *Neue Gedichte* which come close to revealing some of Rilke's own inner existence, his own almost humorously masked and metamorphosed sense of himself, as in that remarkable poem 'The Adventurer', which also conveys something of the artist's awareness of his own lack of substance in the face of the reality of the world which he is trying to penetrate and reveal. 'As he went about among the real/(he, so urgent, who could only *seem*)', he behaves with exquisite address to duchesses, not altogether unlike the manner in which Rilke himself behaved in the world. Rilke was no Don Juan, but he could well understand how a Don Juan might feel:

> His slender body grew, became the bow
> no female hands would find the strength to force.
> Often a look of interest would flow
> across his features, then it would pass
>
> and settle on a face he saw: some woman
> from a painting long ago whose strangeness
> made him smile. He had outgrown
> that darkness he had filled with childhood's tears
>
> and felt at ease and now began to use
> a self-assurance that reached just too far:
> he gravely met the test of women's eyes
> admiring him and setting him on fire.

It is not too difficult to translate a poem in such a way that we can get the *point* of it. But Rilke's poetry does not have a point in quite this sense. Its 'point', however subtle, can be got across in another language and grasped by the reader, but the whole aura of his verse, on which it

18

depends, usually will not accompany it: hence the impression made by the verse is in some way misleading, not right, however verbally accurate the rendering may be. In 'Don Juan's Childhood', to take just one example, the translator has managed not only to convey Rilke's penetrating sense of what it would be like to be a Don Juan in childhood, but also – a far more difficult task – the quality of poetic speech which is unique to this particular poem, and which supplies a kind of code in which the poet seems to be conversing with his subject, and miraculously making it intelligible to us in the process.

It is this image of a code, the code which is the outward and visible sign of Rilke's personality, which must be found for Rilke in an alternative linguistic situation. Nothing could be more personal than Rilke's approach, whether it is to the rose window at Chartres, or to the story of Saint Sebastian, a blue hydrangea, a portrait of his father as a young man, a morning in Venice, a woman playing the piano. In order to give these things to themselves, to show them to us like the flowers which, as he says, seem endlessly to prolong themselves into their own atmosphere, Rilke endows them with the tender exactness of his own speech, his blend of language into being. Certainly Rilke has never 'moved' so naturally into another language as he seems to do in Stephen Cohn's renderings of these poems. The thing has a deceptive ease about it, as with all really remarkable achievements in the translation of poetry. Instead of feeling, as Robert Frost famously said, that poetry is what gets lost when a poem is translated, we feel that not only has Rilke emerged in English with his personality unaltered, but that something new has been added to English poetry itself.

John Bayley

NEUE GEDICHTE I

Karl und Elisabeth von der Heydt
in Freundschaft

FRÜHER APOLLO

Wie manches Mal durch das noch unbelaubte
   Gezweig ein Morgen durchsieht, der schon ganz
im Frühling ist: so ist in seinem Haupte
nichts was verhindern könnte, daß der Glanz

aller Gedichte uns fast tödlich träfe;
denn noch kein Schatten ist in seinem Schaun,
zu kühl für Lorbeer sind noch seine Schläfe
und später erst wird aus den Augenbraun

hochstämmig sich der Rosengarten heben,
aus welchem Blätter, einzeln, ausgelöst
hintreiben werden auf des Mundes Beben,

der jetzt noch still ist, niegebraucht und blinkend
und nur mit seinem Lächeln etwas trinkend
als würde ihm sein Singen eingeflößt.

MÄDCHEN-KLAGE

Diese Neigung, in den Jahren,
   da wir alle Kinder waren,
viel allein zu sein, war mild;
andern ging die Zeit im Streite,
und man hatte seine Seite,
seine Nähe, seine Weite,
einen Weg, ein Tier, ein Bild.

Und ich dachte noch, das Leben
hörte niemals auf zu geben,
daß man sich in sich besinnt.
Bin ich in mir nicht im Größten?
Will mich Meines nicht mehr trösten
und verstehen wie als Kind?

Early Apollo

Sometimes a morning that is sheerest Spring
may peer through twigs still bare of foliage:
nothing obscures his head and nothing screens
us from this almost fatal radiance

of all poems ever, of all poetry.
For there is yet no shadow in his gaze,
his brow is still too fresh for laurel wreaths
and time must pass before the long-stemmed rose

can flourish at his eyebrows and put out
and open, one by one, its tender leaves
to touch and to caress the trembling mouth

that is still shining-new, still motionless;
lips smiling, open as if drinking,
as if to drink the liquid of his song.

A Girl's Lament

In those years that we were children
being solitary pleased us.
Others wasted days in faction:
we had our own near and distant
places, we possessed our stories,
our own pictures, pathways, creatures.

I was certain then our lives
could not ever cease from showing
means for us to know ourselves;
in ourselves were we not sovereign –
comprehending, like all children,
what was ours and reassuring?
All at once that spell was broken

Plötzlich bin ich wie verstoßen,
und zu einem Übergroßen
wird mir diese Einsamkeit,
wenn, auf meiner Brüste Hügeln
stehend, mein Gefühl nach Flügeln
oder einem Ende schreit.

LIEBES-LIED

Wie soll ich meine Seele halten, daß
sie nicht an deine rührt? Wie soll ich sie
hinheben über dich zu andern Dingen?
Ach gerne möcht ich sie bei irgendwas
Verlorenem im Dunkel unterbringen
an einer fremden stillen Stelle, die
nicht weiterschwingt, wenn deine Tiefen schwingen.
Doch alles, was uns anrührt, dich und mich,
nimmt uns zusammen wie ein Bogenstrich,
der aus zwei Saiten *eine* Stimme zieht.
Auf welches Instrument sind wir gespannt?
Und welcher Geiger hat uns in der Hand?
O süßes Lied.

ERANNA AN SAPPHO

O du wilde weite Werferin:
Wie ein Speer bei andern Dingen
lag ich bei den Meinen. Dein Erklingen
warf mich weit. Ich weiß nicht *wo* ich bin.
Mich kann keiner wiederbringen.

and I felt cast out, an exile
in a solitude grown monstrous,
hearing all my senses cry
from their hill-top, from my breasts:
Give us wings or let us die!

Love Song

How might I keep my soul from touching yours?
How should I try to set it free,
to lift it higher? How willingly
I'd hide it in some foreign, distant place,
in darkness, silence; among desolate things
that would not answer when your spirit sings.

All that can touch on us, myself and you,
draws us together as a fiddler's bow
playing upon two strings can draw one sound:
upon what instrument have we been strung?
And what musician holds us in his hand?
How sweet the song!

Eranna to Sappho

Javelin-thrower, champion, wild one!
You first chanced on me, forgotten,
like a javelin in the clutter
of our household: you exclaimed
and hurled me; I fell far beyond direction
...Who will ever fetch me back again?

25

Meine Schwestern denken mich und weben,
und das Haus ist voll vertrauter Schritte.
Ich allein bin fern und fortgegeben,
und ich zittere wie eine Bitte;
denn die schöne Göttin in der Mitte
ihrer Mythen glüht und lebt mein Leben.

SAPPHO AN ERANNA

Unruh will ich über dich bringen,
schwingen will ich dich, umrankter Stab.
Wie das Sterben will ich dich durchdringen
und dich weitergeben wie das Grab
an das Alles: allen diesen Dingen.

SAPPHO AN ALKAÏOS
FRAGMENT

Und was hättest du mir denn zu sagen,
und was gehst du meine Seele an,
wenn sich deine Augen niederschlagen
vor dem nahen Nichtgesagten? Mann,

sieh, uns hat das Sagen dieser Dinge
hingerissen und bis in den Ruhm.
Wenn ich denke: unter euch verginge
dürftig unser süßes Mädchentum,

welches wir, ich Wissende und jene
mit mir Wissenden, vom Gott bewacht,
trugen unberührt, daß Mytilene
wie ein Apfelgarten in der Nacht
duftete vom Wachsen unsrer Brüste –.

Back at home my memory haunts my sisters
at their looms; trusted footsteps, voices!
Far from them I tremble like a plea,
for the lovely legendary Goddess
glows, alive, and lives my life for me.

Sappho to Eranna

Unrest I shall bring you, violence,
    shake you like a stake the vine had smothered.
Like a death I shall pierce through you.
Like the grave transmit your essence
into all things, everywhere, forever.

Sappho to Alcaeus
(a fragment)

What could there still remain for you to say,
    you with the downcast eyes who turn aside?
What could my spirit find to share with you
who leave the things which touch us all unsaid?

For see! the very speaking of our love
uplifted us and raised us into glory:
how much the poorer we should be, how starved,
wasting our maiden years away among you –

years all of us who were initiates
continued to preserve in chastity
protected by the God, till like an orchard's
breath a perfume scented Mytilene:
the fragrance of the flowering of our breasts –

Ja, auch dieser Brüste, die du nicht
wähltest wie zu Fruchtgewinden, Freier
mit dem weggesenkten Angesicht.
Geh und laß mich, daß zu meiner Leier
komme, was du abhältst: alles steht.

Dieser Gott ist nicht der Beistand Zweier,
aber wenn er durch den Einen geht
– –

GRABMAL EINES JUNGEN MÄDCHENS

Wir gedenkens noch. Das ist, als müßte
alles dieses einmal wieder sein.
Wie ein Baum an der Limonenküste
trugst du deine kleinen leichten Brüste
in das Rauschen seines Bluts hinein:

– jenes Gottes.
                    Und es war der schlanke
Flüchtling, der Verwöhnende der Fraun.
Süß und glühend, warm wie dein Gedanke,
überschattend deine frühe Flanke
und geneigt wie deine Augenbraun.

OPFER

O wie blüht mein Leib aus jeder Ader
duftender, seitdem ich dich erkenn;
sieh, ich gehe schlanker und gerader,
und du wartest nur –: wer bist du denn?

of breasts like these you did not wish to choose
to make your garland, you who turn your face
aside; even from her you woo.
Depart and leave me! for my lyre craves
what you cannot provide. Your heart stays free.

This God will never pledge himself to two,
but when by choice he enters into one
– –

Epitaph for a Young Girl

We still remember, for it is as if
a time must come when all will be renewed.
Like a tree growing among lemon-groves
you offered up the brightness of your breasts
which he took deep into his singing blood.

Did you not recognise that slippery god,
the pleasurer of women and their joy?
As sweet, as ardent as your own desires
he cast his shadow on your youthfulness,
curved over you, as slender as a bow.

Offering

Every part of my body, every vein
breaks into blossom, blooms luxuriantly;
walking more upright, seeming leaner, lighter;
meanwhile you wait for me...who are you then?

Sieh: ich fühle, wie ich mich entferne,
wie ich Altes, Blatt um Blatt, verlier.
Nur dein Lächeln steht wie lauter Sterne
über dir und bald auch über mir.

Alles was durch meine Kinderjahre
namenlos noch und wie Wasser glänzt,
will ich nach dir nennen am Altare,
der entzündet ist von deinem Haare
und mit deinen Brüsten leicht bekränzt.

ÖSTLICHES TAGLIED

Ist dieses Bette nicht wie eine Küste,
ein Küstenstreifen nur, darauf wir liegen?
Nichts ist gewiß als deine hohen Brüste,
die mein Gefühl in Schwindeln überstiegen.

Denn diese Nacht, in der so vieles schrie,
in der sich Tiere rufen und zerreißen,
ist sie uns nicht entsetzlich fremd? Und wie:
was draußen langsam anhebt, Tag geheißen,
ist das uns denn verständlicher als sie?

Man müßte so sich ineinanderlegen
wie Blütenblätter um die Staubgefäße:
so sehr ist überall das Ungemäße
und häuft sich an und stürzt sich uns entgegen.

Doch während wir uns aneinander drücken,
um nicht zu sehen, wie es ringsum naht,
kann es aus dir, kann es aus mir sich zücken:
denn unsre Seelen leben von Verrat.

Little by little, see how I depart
from my old customs, shed them leaf by leaf;
only your smile stays constant, pure as starlight
carrying brightness now at last to me.

Those nameless marvels, wonders of my childhood,
shining as sunlight shines on moving water
I dedicate to you, lay on the altar
brightly illuminated by your hair
and garlanded with beauty by your breasts.

Oriental Aubade

Within this bed, is this not like a coast?
a narrow slip of land on which we lie,
the only certainties your high, firm breasts
and all my senses dizzy with desire?

The night, its sounds, the voices of its creatures,
the cries of fiercely-ravening animals –
how terrible and strange it seems to us:
when gradually what we call day appears
is it not (just as night) unknowable?

Better if we could always lie as close
as petals to the stamens in a flower,
hidden from the violent frenzy everywhere
increasing, battering, threatening us.

But even as we press together tightly
and keep the crowding menace from our eyes,
it maybe hides in you or hides in me
because our spirits live by treachery.

ABISAG

I

S ie lag. Und ihre Kinderarme waren
   von Dienern um den Welkenden gebunden,
auf dem sie lag die süßen langen Stunden,
ein wenig bang vor seinen vielen Jahren.

Und manchmal wandte sie in seinem Barte
ihr Angesicht, wenn eine Eule schrie;
und alles, was die Nacht war, kam und scharte
mit Bangen und Verlangen sich um sie.

Die Sterne zitterten wie ihresgleichen,
ein Duft ging suchend durch das Schlafgemach,
der Vorhang rührte sich und gab ein Zeichen,
und leise ging ihr Blick dem Zeichen nach –.

Aber sie hielt sich an dem dunkeln Alten
und, von der Nacht der Nächte nicht erreicht,
lag sie auf seinem fürstlichen Erkalten
jungfräulich und wie eine Seele leicht.

II

D er König saß und sann den leeren Tag
   getaner Taten, ungefühlter Lüste
und seiner Lieblingshündin, der er pflag –.
Aber am Abend wölbte Abisag
sich über ihm. Sein wirres Leben lag
verlassen wie verrufne Meeresküste
unter dem Sternbild ihrer stillen Brüste.

Und manchmal, als ein Kundiger der Frauen,
erkannte er durch seine Augenbrauen
den unbewegten, küsselosen Mund;
und sah: ihres Gefühles grüne Rute
neigte sich nicht herab zu seinem Grund.
Ihn fröstelte. Er horchte wie ein Hund
und suchte sich in seinem letzten Blute.

Abishag

I

She lay above him. Endless, tender hours.
Attendants had arranged her childish arms
around the withered king. She felt afraid
before the awesome mountain of his years.

Sometimes a shrieking owl would startle her:
she hid against the reassuring beard
when the whole night came crowding, pressing in,
heavy with anxious longings and with fears.

She seemed to tremble with the trembling stars.
A scent came seeking, drifting, through the room.
The curtain moved. It was some kind of sign.
She watched it move. She followed with her gaze.

But still untried and uninitiate
she held herself against his princely coldness
and kept her youth against his darkening age,
innocent and light as any spirit.

II

And cosseting the dog, his favourite bitch,
his deeds all done, his pleasures undesired
the king sat brooding. Day on empty day.
The nights belonged to Abishag. The girl
spread out above him, his wild history lay
forgotten as an unfrequented shore
beneath the quiet starscape of her breasts.

Not ignorant of women, unobserved,
from underneath his brow he spied on her:
he watched her mouth, unkissed and self-secure,
and knew for certain no attraction could
make her green hazel bend to his dry ground.
So cold, so cold; attentive as a hound
he sought for selfhood in his failing blood.

DAVID SINGT VOR SAUL

I

König, hörst du, wie mein Saitenspiel
Fernen wirft, durch die wir uns bewegen:
Sterne treiben uns verwirrt entgegen,
und wir fallen endlich wie ein Regen,
und es blüht, wo dieser Regen fiel.

Mädchen blühen, die du noch erkannt,
die jetzt Frauen sind und mich verführen;
den Geruch der Jungfraun kannst du spüren,
und die Knaben stehen, angespannt
schlank und atmend, an verschwiegnen Türen.

Daß mein Klang dir alles wiederbrächte.
Aber trunken taumelt mein Getön:
Deine Nächte, König, deine Nächte –,
und wie waren, die dein Schaffen schwächte,
o wie waren alle Leiber schön.

Dein Erinnern glaub ich zu begleiten,
weil ich ahne. Doch auf welchen Saiten
greif ich dir ihr dunkles Lustgestöhn? –

II

König, der du alles dieses hattest
und der du mit lauter Leben mich
überwältigest und überschattest:
komm aus deinem Throne und zerbrich
meine Harfe, die du so ermattest.

Sie ist wie ein abgenommner Baum:
durch die Zweige, die dir Frucht getragen,
schaut jetzt eine Tiefe wie von Tagen
welche kommen –, und ich kenn sie kaum.

David Sings before Saul

I

King: do you hear the music of my strings
project a space we move in like our own?
The stars reel past us in confusion
until at last we fall to earth like rain
and everywhere that rain brings flowering.

The girls in flower, still girls in your mind
though grown to women, fill me with desire.
A maiden-perfume whispers on the air
and in the hopeful doorways young men stand
silent and avid, waiting breathless there.

Oh! that my song might give you back those days –
the notes are slurred, it wavers out of tune.
Recall the nights, O King, recall how they
transported you, sapped all your energy!
How beautiful were all their bodies then.

My premonitions guide and shape my songs
to match your memories: where are the strings
to make the darkness sound those sighs again?

II

King: since your own life has possessed
such riches piled on riches rising up
and overwhelming, matchless, in excess –
descend your throne and shatter the poor harp
your shining has made seem so lustreless.

Your servant's harp is like a tree picked clean;
between the branches which bore fruit for you
there shine dimensions that I scarcely know
of music not yet heard, of days unseen.

Laß mich nicht mehr bei der Harfe schlafen;
sieh dir diese Knabenhand da an:
glaubst du, König, daß sie die Oktaven
eines Leibes noch nicht greifen kann?

III

König, birgst du dich in Finsternissen,
und ich hab dich doch in der Gewalt.
Sieh, mein festes Lied ist nicht gerissen,
und der Raum wird um uns beide kalt.
Mein verwaistes Herz und dein verworrnes
hängen in den Wolken deines Zornes,
wütend ineinander eingebissen
und zu einem einzigen verkrallt.

Fühlst du jetzt, wie wir uns umgestalten?
König, König, das Gewicht wird Geist.
Wenn wir uns nur aneinander halten,
du am Jungen, König, ich am Alten,
sind wir fast wie ein Gestirn das kreist.

JOSUAS LANDTAG

So wie der Strom am Ausgang seine Dämme
durchbricht mit seiner Mündung Übermaß,
so brach nun durch die Ältesten der Stämme
zum letzten Mal die Stimme Josuas.

Wie waren die geschlagen, welche lachten,
wie hielten alle Herz und Hände an,
als hübe sich der Lärm von dreißig Schlachten
in einem Mund; und dieser Mund begann.

Und wieder waren Tausende voll Staunen
wie an dem großen Tag vor Jericho,
nun aber waren in ihm die Posaunen,
und ihres Lebens Mauern schwankten so,

King, look upon this youthful hand:
must I sleep with my harp in this cold place?
Can you believe, King, that I cannot span
the octaves of a woman's nakedness?

III

King: though you hide yourself in darkness
you still cannot escape my music's force.
While the dark room grows cold as dew for us
my song, inviolable, feels no distress.
Both trapped in the dark cloud of your frustration,
my orphaned heart, your heart full of confusion,
each in their rage devouring the other
unite and fuse in angry bitterness.

King, *spirit* is the child of melancholy.
King, can you feel how changed we are?
Welded together in this unity,
while my youth cleaves to your maturity,
we shall resemble one great circling star.

Joshua's Ordinance

A torrent at its outflow breaches dams
to thunder on into the estuary:
the elders of the tribes for one more time
are audience to Joshua's oratory.

They listen and contain their hearts and hands.
Any who dare to scoff are stilled with blows.
From that one mouth as, roaring, he began,
a roar like that of thirty battles rose

so that they marvelled, just as once before
on that triumphant day at Jericho.
His voice alone now made the trumpets roar
and shook the ramparts of their lives, so

daß sie sich wälzten von Entsetzen trächtig
und wehrlos schon und überwältigt, eh
sie's noch gedachten, wie er eigenmächtig
zu Gibeon die Sonne anschrie: steh!

Und Gott ging hin, erschrocken wie ein Knecht,
und hielt die Sonne, bis ihm seine Hände
wehtaten, ob dem schlachtenden Geschlecht,
nur weil da einer wollte, daß sie stände.

Und das war dieser; dieser Alte wars,
von dem sie meinten, daß er nicht mehr gelte
inmitten seines hundertzehnten Jahrs.
Da stand er auf und brach in ihre Zelte.

Er ging wie Hagel nieder über Halmen:
Was wollt ihr Gott versprechen? Ungezählt
stehn um euch Götter, wartend daß ihr wählt.
Doch wenn ihr wählt, wird euch der Herr zermalmen.

Und dann, mit einem Hochmut ohnegleichen:
Ich und mein Haus, wir bleiben ihm vermählt.

Da schrien sie alle: Hilf uns, gib ein Zeichen
und stärke uns zu unsrer schweren Wahl.

Aber sie sahn ihn, wie seit Jahren schweigend,
zu seiner festen Stadt am Berge steigend;
und dann nicht mehr. Es war das letzte Mal.

that they quaked and trembled and were filled with dread,
disarmed and overwhelmed. Now they recalled
the solitary voice at Gibeon, how it had cried
to halt the circling sun and bellowed: Hold!

and God, Himself alarmed, had seized the sun
when like a servant He had hastened there,
held it until His hands began to burn,
for one man's sake, while they had fought their war.

And it was he. That was this same old man.
They thought him spent, of little consequence
now he was aged one hundred years and ten,
and like a fire he rages in their tents!

He hammered down like hail on tender corn:
What will you pledge the Lord? for numberless
legions of gods wait and attend your choice.
But when you choose, the Lord shall smite you down.

Then with incomparable pride he said:
My house and I espouse none but the Lord.

And all cried out: Send us some sign. Help us
and strengthen us to make this heavy choice.

They saw him turn and once again resume
the silence he had worn for years, and climb
the steep track to his stronghold, the last time.

Nun fortzugehn von alledem Verworrnen,
das unser ist und uns doch nicht gehört,
das, wie das Wasser in den alten Bornen,
uns zitternd spiegelt und das Bild zerstört;
von allem diesen, das sich wie mit Dornen
noch einmal an uns anhängt – fortzugehn
und Das und Den,
die man schon nicht mehr sah
(so täglich waren sie und so gewöhnlich),
auf einmal anzuschauen: sanft, versöhnlich
und wie an einem Anfang und von nah;
und ahnend einzusehn, wie unpersönlich,
wie über alle hin das Leid geschah,
von dem die Kindheit voll war bis zum Rand –:
Und dann doch fortzugehen, Hand aus Hand,
als ob man ein Geheiltes neu zerrisse,
und fortzugehn: wohin? Ins Ungewisse,
weit in ein unverwandtes warmes Land,
das hinter allem Handeln wie Kulisse
gleichgültig sein wird: Garten oder Wand;
und fortzugehn: warum? Aus Drang, aus Artung,
aus Ungeduld, aus dunkeler Erwartung,
aus Unverständlichkeit und Unverstand:

Dies alles auf sich nehmen und vergebens
vielleicht Gehaltnes fallen lassen, um
allein zu sterben, wissend nicht warum –

Ist das der Eingang eines neuen Lebens?

DER ÖLBAUM-GARTEN

Er ging hinauf unter dem grauen Laub
ganz grau und aufgelöst im Ölgelände
und legte seine Stirne voller Staub
tief in das Staubigsein der heißen Hände.

The Departure of the Prodigal Son

At last to leave behind all that confusion:
the things of ours that never quite belonged
although, like water in a well, they served
to reflect ourselves (it trembled: we were gone);
to shed what still attempts to cling
as if attached by thorns – and suddenly
to see in close-up, every detail clear,
people and things impossible to see
(familiar and banal and always there)
and find them tender and conciliatory;
at last to comprehend old injuries
and realise how disproportionate
our childhood's overwhelming sense of hurt
had been; in spite of all to leave, to tear
our hands away as if to tear a scar
already healed, and to depart: but where?
Into uncertainty, looking to find
some distant, unfamiliar, temperate land
to be the setting that our actions need
(the courtyard, or the garden, as required);
to take our leave: but why? Because we're driven;
because of what we are, our dispositions;
because of urgent premonitions;
because of darkness and our lack of vision:

To make this whole attempt; perhaps in vain
let go of what we hold; perhaps to die
uncomprehendingly, perhaps alone –
How else can we discover a new life?

The Garden of Olives

He went up, in the shade of the grey leaves,
grey lost in greyness in the olive-lands,
letting his dusty forehead find some ease
in the hot dustiness of his own hands.

41

Nach allem dies. Und dieses war der Schluß.
Jetzt soll ich gehen, während ich erblinde,
und warum willst Du, daß ich sagen muß
Du seist, wenn ich Dich selber nicht mehr finde.

Ich finde Dich nicht mehr. Nicht in mir, nein.
Nicht in den andern. Nicht in diesem Stein.
Ich finde Dich nicht mehr. Ich bin allein.

Ich bin allein mit aller Menschen Gram,
den ich durch Dich zu lindern unternahm,
der Du nicht bist. O namenlose Scham…

Später erzählte man: ein Engel kam –.

Warum ein Engel? Ach es kam die Nacht
und blätterte gleichgültig in den Bäumen.
Die Jünger rührten sich in ihren Träumen.
Warum ein Engel? Ach es kam die Nacht.

Die Nacht, die kam, war keine ungemeine;
so gehen hunderte vorbei.
Da schlafen Hunde und da liegen Steine.
Ach eine traurige, ach irgendeine,
die wartet, bis es wieder Morgen sei.

Denn Engel kommen nicht zu solchen Betern,
und Nächte werden nicht um solche groß.
Die Sich-Verlierenden läßt alles los,
und sie sind preisgegeben von den Vätern
und ausgeschlossen aus der Mütter Schooß.

PIETÀ

S o seh ich, Jesus, deine Füße wieder,
die damals eines Jünglings Füße waren,
da ich sie bang entkleidete und wusch;
wie standen sie verwirrt in meinen Haaren
und wie ein weißes Wild im Dornenbusch.

My sight grows dim. Now I must go my way.
Now all is over – is this how it ends?
How can You still require me to say;
He is? for even I no longer find

You anywhere – I seek but You are gone,
gone from all men, all women, from this stone.
I find You nowhere. Now I am alone.

I am alone with all mankind's distress
which You could help me heal – it was my promise.
You who are not – Your silence my disgrace!

Then, people said, an Angel from the skies –

There was no Angel. What came then was night
and unconcerned it stirred the trees and rustled
among the dreams dreamed by the young disciples.
There was no Angel. Nothing came but night

and night was commonplace in every way,
no different from a hundred nights that pass
whose dogs must sleep, whose stones lie quietly;
a night of darkness, not extraordinary,
it waited for the morning sun to rise.

Angels will answer none who pray such prayers
nor will the night make Revelation come:
the self-abandoned are themselves abandoned
and shall be cast out even by the fathers –
forever banished from the mother's womb.

Pietà

Again, Lord, for a second time I know
the feet I touched when you and they were young.
I washed their dust away and saw them shine
like shy white creatures, caught and held among
my tumbled hair as if ensnared by thorns.

43

So seh ich deine niegeliebten Glieder
zum erstenmal in dieser Liebesnacht.
Wir legten uns noch nie zusammen nieder,
und nun wird nur bewundert und gewacht.

Doch, siehe, deine Hände sind zerrissen –:
Geliebter, nicht von mir, von meinen Bissen.
Dein Herz steht offen und man kann hinein:
das hätte dürfen nur mein Eingang sein.

Nun bist du müde, und dein müder Mund
hat keine Lust zu meinem wehen Munde –.
O Jesus, Jesus, wann war unsre Stunde?
Wie gehn wir beide wunderlich zugrund.

GESANG DER FRAUEN AN DEN DICHTER

Sieh, wie sich alles auftut: so sind wir;
denn wir sind nichts als solche Seligkeit.
Was Blut und Dunkel war in einem Tier,
das wuchs in uns zur Seele an und schreit

als Seele weiter. Und es schreit nach dir.
Du freilich nimmst es nur in dein Gesicht
als sei es Landschaft: sanft und ohne Gier.
Und darum meinen wir, du bist es nicht,

nach dem es schreit. Und doch, bist du nicht der,
an den wir uns ganz ohne Rest verlören?
Und werden wir in irgendeinem *mehr*?

Mit uns geht das Unendliche *vorbei*.
Du aber sei, du Mund, daß wir es hören,
du aber, du Uns-Sagender: du sei.

Again I see your limbs that never knew
their lover's touch; tonight I hold them fast.
Craving you always, I may hold you now.
Amazed, awake, I lie with you at last.

Your heart stands open. Any may go in
where there should be a place for me alone.
And, see! your wounded hands, far better they
had felt the sharpness of my teeth in play.

I feel your weariness. Your weary mouth
feels no desire for my grieving mouth.
How strange a way for us to meet our end!
Lord, could no time, no place for us be found?

The Women Sing to the Poet

See how the whole World flowers: so do we!
The darkly-moving blood of animals
is changed within ourselves into a soul –
at heart we are pure spirit, joyful, free,

which in a spirit-voice cries out to *you*.
You turn to us and unpossessively
contemplate us – as you'd admire a view.
We have no choice: we must reluctantly

conclude it was not you our spirits cried for.
Who was it, then, to whom our hearts were lost
beyond recall – who could have given us more?

Eternity for us is transitory –
but you can speak for us and witness it!
You speak ourselves – speak *us* and never die!

45

Er lag. Sein aufgestelltes Antlitz war
bleich und verweigernd in den steilen Kissen,
seitdem die Welt und dieses von-ihr-Wissen,
von seinen Sinnen abgerissen,
zurückfiel an das teilnahmslose Jahr.

Die, so ihn leben sahen, wußten nicht,
wie sehr er Eines war mit allem diesen;
denn Dieses: diese Tiefen, diese Wiesen
und diese Wasser *waren* sein Gesicht.

O sein Gesicht war diese ganze Weite,
die jetzt noch zu ihm will und um ihn wirbt;
und seine Maske, die nun bang verstirbt,
ist zart und offen wie die Innenseite
von einer Frucht, die an der Luft verdirbt.

BUDDHA

Als ob er horchte. Stille: eine Ferne…
Wir halten ein und hören sie nicht mehr.
Und er ist Stern. Und andre große Sterne,
die wir nicht sehen, stehen um ihn her.

O er ist Alles. Wirklich, warten wir,
daß er uns sähe? Sollte er bedürfen?
Und wenn wir hier uns vor ihm niederwürfen,
er bliebe tief und träge wie ein Tier.

Denn das, was uns zu seinen Füßen reißt,
das kreist in ihm seit Millionen Jahren.
Er, der vergißt was wir erfahren
und der erfährt was uns verweist.

The Poet's Death

He lies like something on display, the pale
forbidding face propped on high pillows,
sense-of-the-world entirely wrenched away,
life's taste, its smell gone irretrievably.
Nature, unmoved, accommodates it all.

None who had watched him living could have known
how with its waters, valleys, meadows
the world and he were genuinely one:
he *was* these things, they had been his true face,

drawn towards him, alive around him yet,
and their expansiveness made up his features.
Only his mask is vulnerable and dies,
fragile and perishable like fruits
whose inwardness, exposed, at once decays.

Buddha

As if he were an ear for silence, space.
We have stopped listening. We no longer hear.
He is a star, and many a giant star
stands all about him though unseen by us.
Oh, he is all things. Is our destiny
only to await his need for us at last?
If we abased ourselves before him he
would stay unmoved, as distant as a beast.

For all the force that drives us to his feet
has worked in him for millions of years.
All that we call experience he can ignore –
experiencing all that shuts us out.

L'ANGE DU MÉRIDIEN

Im Sturm, der um die starke Kathedrale
wie ein Verneiner stürzt der denkt und denkt,
fühlt man sich zärtlicher mit einem Male
von deinem Lächeln zu dir hingelenkt:

lächelnder Engel, fühlende Figur,
mit einem Mund, gemacht aus hundert Munden:
gewahrst du gar nicht, wie dir unsre Stunden
abgleiten von der vollen Sonnenuhr,

auf der des Tages ganze Zahl zugleich,
gleich wirklich, steht in tiefem Gleichgewichte,
als wären alle Stunden reif und reich?

Was weißt du, Steinerner, von unserm Sein?
und hältst du mit noch seligerm Gesichte
vielleicht die Tafel in die Nacht hinein?

DIE KATHEDRALE

In jenen kleinen Städten, wo herum
die alten Häuser wie ein Jahrmarkt hocken,
der *sie* bemerkt hat plötzlich und, erschrocken,
die Buden zumacht und, ganz zu und stumm,

die Schreier still, die Trommeln angehalten,
zu ihr hinaufhorcht aufgeregten Ohrs –:
dieweil sie ruhig immer in dem alten
Faltenmantel ihrer Contreforts
dasteht und von den Häusern gar nicht weiß:

L'Ange du Méridien
Chartres

A round the unassailable cathedral
the storm-wind broods and contradicts and rails
by contrast making irresistible
the affirmation of your gentle smile...

Angel: your stony flesh was taught to feel,
your smiling mouth outwarms a hundred smiles,
but do you watch the overburdened dial
from which the shadows of our hours spill?

With each day's sum of hours engraved on it
and with those hours guaranteed to be
all real, all ripe, and all of equal weight.

Stone Angel: can you learn the human heart?
And do you smile even more joyfully
when no-one reads your tablet but the Night?

The Cathedral

I n those small cities ancient houses sit
like fairground booths. When they catch sight of it
they are alarmed and quickly all is shut
and must stay motionless and deathly-quiet,

the hucksters silenced and the drummers still:
the houses crouch and listen with anxious ears
although it stays oblivious the while
wearing the folds of its grey buttresses
like some old coat; not sparing them a glance.

in jenen kleinen Städten kannst du sehn,
wie sehr entwachsen ihrem Umgangskreis
die Kathedralen waren. Ihr Erstehn
ging über alles fort, so wie den Blick
des eignen Lebens viel zu große Nähe
fortwährend übersteigt, und als geschähe
nichts anderes; als wäre Das Geschick,
was sich in ihnen aufhäuft ohne Maßen,
versteinert und zum Dauernden bestimmt,
nicht Das, was unten in den dunklen Straßen
vom Zufall irgendwelche Namen nimmt
und darin geht, wie Kinder Grün und Rot
und was der Krämer hat als Schürze tragen.
Da war Geburt in diesen Unterlagen,
und Kraft und Andrang war in diesem Ragen
und Liebe überall wie Wein und Brot,
und die Portale voller Liebesklagen.
Das Leben zögerte im Stundenschlagen,
und in den Türmen, welche voll Entsagen
auf einmal nicht mehr stiegen, war der Tod.

DAS PORTAL

I

Da blieben sie, als wäre jene Flut
zurückgetreten, deren großes Branden
an diesen Steinen wusch, bis sie entstanden;
sie nahm im Fallen manches Attribut

aus ihren Händen, welche viel zu gut
und geben sind, um etwas festzuhalten.
Sie blieben, von den Formen in Basalten
durch einen Nimbus, einen Bischofshut,

You see in those old cities just how far
cathedrals must outgrow their ambience,
claiming their own priority before
all else – just as we do when we,
too close to self, see no needs but our own –
as if what grew in them, in them alone,
beyond proportion, teasing gravity,
translated into stone forever to
endure, were Destiny itself, all *this*
and never *that*, among mean streets below,
picking its names somehow from randomness –
like children, red or green perforce
because they wear the smock the draper chose!

Built into its foundations was all birth;
its elevation built by thrust, by growth;
and love like bread and wine was everywhere
and love's distress was heard at every door.

Life faltered at its striking of the hours
and the renunciation of its towers
when all at once they ceased to climb was death.

The Cathedral Porch

I

T hey have been set there as if left behind
by the gigantic forces of the tides
which carved them out and then again retreated
but generous and lavish, openhanded,

left attributes to them which were the sea's;
they are distinguished from the natural
configurations of the rock because
they wear a bishop's mitre or a halo

bisweilen durch ein Lächeln unterschieden,
für das ein Antlitz seiner Stunden Frieden
bewahrt hat als ein stilles Zifferblatt;

jetzt fortgerückt ins Leere ihres Tores,
waren sie einst die Muschel eines Ohres
und fingen jedes Stöhnen dieser Stadt.

II

Sehr viele Weite ist gemeint damit:
so wie mit den Kulissen einer Szene
die Welt gemeint ist; und so wie durch jene
der Held im Mantel seiner Handlung tritt: –

so tritt das Dunkel dieses Tores handelnd
auf seiner Tiefe tragisches Theater,
so grenzenlos und wallend wie Gott-Vater
und so wie Er sich wunderlich verwandelnd

in einen Sohn, der aufgeteilt ist hier
auf viele kleine beinah stumme Rollen,
genommen aus des Elends Zubehör.

Denn nur noch so ensteht (das wissen wir)
aus Blinden, Fortgeworfenen und Tollen
der Heiland wie ein einziger Akteur.

III

So ragen sie, die Herzen angehalten
(sie stehn auf Ewigkeit und gingen nie);
nur selten tritt aus dem Gefäll der Falten
eine Gebärde, aufrecht, steil wie sie,

und bleibt nach einem halben Schritte stehn
wo die Jahrhunderte sie überholen.
Sie sind im Gleichgewicht auf den Konsolen,
in denen eine Welt, die sie nicht sehn,

or, like a clock with its own time to tell,
a face will sometimes even show a smile –
the sum of all its hoarded, peaceful hours:

once, intricate as ears and listening,
they caught the city's sounds, heard every groan:
they guard the entrance now and keep its shadows.

II

A whole dimension is intended here
as on a stage whose backdrop and whose boards
are understood to represent the World –
which, clothed within his part, the Hero enters:

the darkness of this doorway must support,
upon it and within, a tragedy
as infinitely potent as the Lord
and, like Him, self-translating wonderfully

into a Son whose action is dispersed
among various roles expressing wretchedness,
all of them minor and all taciturn,

in this way gradually to rehearse
among the blind, the cast-off, the insane,
the Saviour in a single part: His own.

III

Their hearts are motionless. They stand so tall,
removed from Time and in Eternity.
Sometimes a gesture upwards, vertical
as they, emerges from the drapery

but is abandoned only half-complete
and overtaken by the centuries
while they stay poised above the carved stone brackets,
on which a teeming world they cannot see

die Welt der Wirrnis, die sie nicht zertraten,
Figur und Tier, wie um sie zu gefährden,
sich krümmt und schüttelt und sie dennoch hält:

weil die Gestalten dort wie Akrobaten
sich nur so zuckend und so wild gebärden,
damit der Stab auf ihrer Stirn nicht fällt.

DIE FENSTERROSE

Da drin: das träge Treten ihrer Tatzen
macht eine Stille, die dich fast verwirrt;
und wie dann plötzlich eine von den Katzen
den Blick an ihr, der hin und wieder irrt,

gewaltsam in ihr großes Auge nimmt, –
den Blick, der, wie von eines Wirbels Kreis
ergriffen, eine kleine Weile schwimmt
und dann versinkt und nichts mehr von sich weiß,

wenn dieses Auge, welches scheinbar ruht,
sich auftut und zusammenschlägt mit Tosen
und ihn hineinreißt bis ins rote Blut –:

So griffen einstmals aus dem Dunkelsein
der Kathedralen große Fensterrosen
ein Herz und rissen es in Gott hinein.

DAS KAPITÄL

Wie sich aus eines Traumes Ausgeburten
aufsteigend aus verwirrendem Gequäl
der nächste Tag erhebt: so gehn die Gurten
der Wölbung aus dem wirren Kapitäl

swarms with a wildness still not trodden down –
of figures, crouching beasts which seem to threaten
or cringe away, which hold them none the less:

they cower and they writhe in such confusion,
like acrobats, performing their contortions
for fear the staff will fall upon their heads.

The Rose Window

I nside, the lazy padding of soft feet
creates a silence, almost stupefies;
then all at once one of the drowsing cats
awakes – and pounces; its enormous eye

seizes the drifting image of that quiet,
which for a little while yet swims around,
before the golden whirlpool sucks at it
and drags it down into oblivion:

just as this eye apparently asleep
gapes open, strikes, and drags its capture deep
into the thunder of its own red blood –

so the rose window in that holy time
within the great cathedral's scented gloom
captured a heart and dragged it up to God.

The Capital

A s dawning day will cancel and destroy
the fevered torments and dark creatures born
of dreams, the ribs of vaulting spring out and away
from the crammed capital with its confusion

55

und lassen drin, gedrängt und rätselhaft
verschlungen, flügelschlagende Geschöpfe:
ihr Zögern und das Plötzliche der Köpfe
und jene starken Blätter, deren Saft

wie Jähzorn steigt, sich schließlich überschlagend
in eine schnellen Geste, die sich ballt
und sich heraushält –: alles aufwärtsjagend,

was immer wieder mit dem Dunkel kalt
herunterfällt, wie Regen Sorge tragend
für dieses alten Wachstums Unterhalt.

GOTT IM MITTELALTER

Und sie hatten Ihn in sich erspart
    und sie wollten, daß er sei und richte,
und sie hängten schließlich wie Gewichte
(zu verhindern seine Himmelfahrt)

an ihn ihrer großen Kathedralen
Last und Masse. Und er sollte nur
über seine grenzenlosen Zahlen
zeigend kreisen und wie eine Uhr

Zeichen geben ihrem Tun und Tagewerk.
Aber plötzlich kam er ganz in Gang,
und die Leute der entsetzten Stadt

ließen ihn, vor seiner Stimme bang,
weitergehn mit ausgehängtem Schlagwerk
und entflohn vor seinem Zifferblatt.

56

of flapping monsters tightly interlaced,
entangled, interwoven, dense, mysterious,
their stony heads abrupt, irresolute;
away from fleshy leaves whose rising juice

ascends like rage which finally bursts out
congealed into a fist, an angry ball,
and thrusting out and upwards forces all

before it, rising up as if to rout
the ever-falling darkness and the pain
which feeds old stones as plants are fed by rain.

God in the Middle Ages

Within their hearts all wanted Him restrained.
They meant Him to be there, to regulate,
eventually they meant to weigh Him down
with great cathedrals of such size and weight

as would prevent Him flying off to heaven.
And all He had to do was to preside
and signify and set His seal upon
the whole of their un-numberable World

which He had made: as if He were a clock
for them, to point, to measure tasks and days.
Then all at once He set Himself to work.

The town turned pale and fled away, appalled;
for when His naked clockwork struck the hours,
they saw His face and saw the time it told.

MORGUE

Da liegen sie bereit, als ob es gälte,
nachträglich eine Handlung zu erfinden,
die mit einander und mit dieser Kälte
sie zu versöhnen weiß und zu verbinden;

denn das ist alles noch wie ohne Schluß.
Was für ein Name hätte in den Taschen
sich finden sollen? An dem Überdruß
um ihren Mund hat man herumgewaschen:

er ging nicht ab; er wurde nur ganz rein.
Die Bärte stehen, noch ein wenig härter,
doch ordentlicher im Geschmack der Wärter,

nur um die Gaffenden nicht anzuwidern.
Die Augen haben hinter ihren Lidern
sich umgewandt und schauen jetzt hinein.

DER GEFANGENE

I

Meine Hand hat nur noch eine
Gebärde, mit der sie verscheucht;
auf die alten Steine
fällt es aus Felsen feucht.

Ich höre nur dieses Klopfen
und mein Herz hält Schritt
mit dem Gehen der Tropfen
und vergeht damit.

Tropften sie doch schneller,
käme doch wieder ein Tier.
Irgendwo war es heller –.
Aber was wissen wir.

58

Morgue

Lying there, they seem to wait as if resolved
that, though belatedly, they must discover
some means by which they may endure this cold
and reach some settlement with one another –

for *this* might last forever, never end.
Did they not once have names, when they wore clothes?
What sort of names? Their faces, gaunt and strained,
are dark with discontent around the mouths,

which will not wash away, though sponged quite clean.
Their beards grow stiffly. Their attendants feel
they look quite neat, unlikely to appal

any among the gaping visitors.
But underneath the eyelids all their eyes
are turned about and now look only inwards.

The Captive

I

My hand now remembers only
to refuse – waves all things back.
Water drips upon old stones,
weeping from the rock.

Drops of moisture falling
my heart keeping pace
echoing their motion
with each droplet, dies.

Must they fall so slowly?
Somewhere once the light was brighter.
How I wish there were some creature...
What is there we know?

Denk dir, das was jetzt Himmel ist und Wind,
Luft deinem Mund und deinem Auge Helle,
das würde Stein bis um die kleine Stelle
an der dein Herz und deine Hände sind.

Und was jetzt in dir morgen heißt und: dann
und: späterhin und nächstes Jahr und weiter –
das würde wund in dir und voller Eiter
und schwäre nur und bräche nicht mehr an.

Und das was war, das wäre irre und
raste in dir herum, den lieben Mund
der niemals lachte, schäumend von Gelächter.

Und das was Gott war, wäre nur dein Wächter
und stopfte boshaft in das letzte Loch
ein schmutziges Auge. Und du lebtest doch.

DER PANTHER
IM JARDIN DES PLANTES, PARIS

Sein Blick ist vom Vorübergehn der Stäbe
so müd geworden, daß er nichts mehr hält.
Ihm ist, als ob es tausend Stäbe gäbe
und hinter tausend Stäben keine Welt.

Der weiche Gang geschmeidig starker Schritte,
der sich im allerkleinsten Kreise dreht,
ist wie ein Tanz von Kraft um eine Mitte,
in der betäubt ein großer Wille steht.

Nur manchmal schiebt der Vorhang der Pupille
sich lautlos auf –. Dann geht ein Bild hinein,
geht durch der Glieder angespannte Stille –
und hört im Herzen auf zu sein.

I magine all around you, skies and wind
  transformed to stone, the whole world petrified,
the breath you breathe, the light within your eyes,
your own small world, your living heart, your hands,

the words that you possess: *this morning, later,
further off, next year* – suppose those words
were to grow painful, were to grow infected
and purulent and never ceased to fester,

and all you know changed crazily about
and the beloved, never-smiling mouth
were seen by you idiotically laughing

and what was once your God became a gaoler
who blocked the last remaining aperture
with his malevolent eye: but you must go on living.

The Panther
Jardin des Plantes, Paris

T he bars which pass and strike across his gaze
  have stunned his sight: the eyes have lost their hold.
To him it seems there are a thousand bars,
a thousand bars and nothing else. No World.

And pacing out that mean, constricted ground,
so quiet, supple, powerful, his stride
is like a ritual dance performed around
the centre where his baffled will survives.

The silent shutter of his eye sometimes
slides open to admit some thing outside;
an image runs through each expectant limb
and penetrates his heart, and dies.

DIE GAZELLE
GAZELLA DORCAS

Verzauberte: wie kann der Einklang zweier
erwählter Worte je den Reim erreichen,
der in dir kommt und geht, wie auf ein Zeichen.
Aus deiner Stirne steigen Laub und Leier,

und alles Deine geht schon im Vergleich
durch Liebeslieder, deren Worte, weich
wie Rosenblätter, dem, der nicht mehr liest,
sich auf die Augen legen, die er schließt:

um dich zu sehen: hingetragen, als
wäre mit Sprüngen jeder Lauf geladen
und schösse nur nicht ab, solang der Hals

das Haupt ins Horchen hält: wie wenn beim Baden
im Wald die Badende sich unterbricht:
den Waldsee im gewendeten Gesicht.

DAS EINHORN

Der Heilige hob das Haupt, und das Gebet
fiel wie ein Helm zurück von seinem Haupte:
denn lautlos nahte sich das niegeglaubte,
das weiße Tier, das wie eine geraubte
hülflose Hindin mit den Augen fleht.

Der Beine elfenbeinernes Gestell
bewegte sich in leichten Gleichgewichten,
ein weißer Glanz glitt selig durch das Fell,
und auf der Tierstirn, auf der stillen, lichten,
stand, wie ein Turm im Mond, das Horn so hell,
und jeder Schritt geschah, es aufzurichten.

The Gazelle
Gazella Dorcas

E nchanted animal: can any sound
from two rhymed words reflect the harmony
which flows through you, as if by alchemy?
Laurel and lyre flourish from your brow,

each feature, every movement, bears
comparison with any love-song, those
words soft as the petals of a rose
which fall on readers' eyes and make them close:

to see you delicately poised upon
legs like the slender barrels of four guns –
which will not shoot while your head still remains

turned on its neck, alertly listening. As
bathing in the woods a girl might turn,
woodland and water shining from her face.

The Unicorn

T he saint looked up from prayer and all the prayers
fell from him, like a helmet to the ground:
before him stood the not-to-be-believed,
the fabulous white creature with the eyes
of some beseeching, helpless, captured hind.

Its legs, four subtle ivory stilts,
advanced in slender equipoise. A soft
white light caressed its shining pelt,
and on the creature's lucent brow the horn:
an ivory spire upon a shining moon.
Each step it made raised that bright horn aloft.

Das Maul mit seinem rosagrauen Flaum
war leicht gerafft, so daß ein wenig Weiß
(weißer als alles) von den Zähnen glänzte;
die Nüstern nahmen auf und lechzten leis.
Doch seine Blicke, die kein Ding begrenzte,
warfen sich Bilder in den Raum
und schlossen einen blauen Sagenkreis.

SANKT SEBASTIAN

Wie ein Liegender so steht er; ganz
hingehalten von dem großen Willen.
Weitentrückt wie Mütter, wenn sie stillen,
und in sich gebunden wie ein Kranz.

Und die Pfeile kommen: jetzt und jetzt
und als sprängen sie aus seinen Lenden,
eisern bebend mit den freien Enden.
Doch er lächelt dunkel, unverletzt.

Einmal nur wird seine Trauer groß,
und die Augen liegen schmerzlich bloß,
bis sie etwas leugnen, wie Geringes,
und als ließen sie verächtlich los
die Vernichter eines schönen Dinges.

DER STIFTER

Das war der Auftrag an die Malergilde.
Vielleicht daß ihm der Heiland nie erschien;
vielleicht trat auch kein heiliger Bischof milde
an seine Seite wie in diesem Bilde
und legte leise seine Hand auf ihn.

The muzzle slightly open: downy grey
and rose; a pearly whiteness where the teeth
just show; the nostrils' even breath.
Nothing withstood the magic of its eyes –
wherever their gaze rested filled with images:
a universe of legendary blue.

Saint Sebastian

O ffered without reserve by his fierce faith
he stands upright as if he lay at rest,
preoccupied as women giving breast,
all wrapped within himself: a human wreath.

Again the arrows swarm, again they fall
and strike and pierce; they quiver there
as if steel shafts had sprouted from his thighs.
He seems, unharmed, mysteriously to smile.

Once only is the anguish evident
and his stark eyes, expressive of the torment
he repudiates, look scornfully
away from those they judge of no account:
men who would vandalise a thing so wonderful.

The Donor

T he picture was commissioned from the Painters'
Guild. We do not know if once the Lord
appeared to him or if a Bishop stood
benignly at his side, or if he gently
laid a hand in blessing on his head.

Vielleicht war dieses alles: *so* zu knien
(so wie es alles ist was wir erfuhren):
zu knien: daß man die eigenen Konturen,
die auswärtswollenden, ganz angespannt
im Herzen hält, wie Pferde in der Hand.

Daß wenn ein Ungeheueres geschähe,
das nicht versprochen ist und nieverbrieft,
wir hoffen könnten, daß es uns nicht sähe
und näher käme, ganz in unsre Nähe,
mit sich beschäftigt und in sich vertieft.

DER ENGEL

M it einem Neigen seiner Stirne weist
er weit von sich was einschränkt und verpflichtet;
denn durch sein Herz geht riesig aufgerichtet
das ewig Kommende, das kreist.

Die tiefen Himmel stehn ihm voll Gestalten,
und jede kann ihm rufen: komm, erkenn –.
Gieb seinen leichten Händen nichts zu halten
aus deinem Lastenden. Sie kämen denn

bei Nacht zu dir, dich ringender zu prüfen,
und gingen wie Erzürnte durch das Haus
und griffen dich als ob sie dich erschüfen
und brächen dich aus deiner Form heraus.

It may be this was all, with no more offered
than this chance to kneel – and maybe this
is all there ever is or was for us:
to kneel and hold our limitations, reined
back like horses, tightly in our hands.

And when something miraculous occurs,
something unheralded, not ever promised,
perhaps we pray that it will simply pass
us by, though it comes very close to us,
deep in its own concerns and self-immersed.

The Angel

He shakes his head as if he would dismiss
whatever might confine him or constrain –
for each gigantic heartbeat brings more close
the huge event – forever orbiting.

All heaven shouts and swarms with presences
ready to summon him: Come! See and witness!
But do not burden with your heaviness
his weightless hands, for they would break your doors

and, raging in the night from room to room,
would seize you and search deep into your heart,
wrench you about as if to give you form –
at last would break your mould, would lift you out.

RÖMISCHE SARKOPHAGE

Was aber hindert uns zu glauben, daß
    (so wie wir hingestellt sind und verteilt)
nicht eine kleine Zeit nur Drang und Haß
und dies Verwirrende in uns verweilt,

wie einst in dem verzierten Sarkophag
bei Ringen, Götterbildern, Gläsern, Bändern,
in langsam sich verzehrenden Gewändern
ein langsam Aufgelöstes lag –

bis es die unbekannten Munde schluckten,
die niemals reden. (Wo besteht und denkt
ein Hirn, um ihrer einst sich zu bedienen?)

Da wurde von den alten Aquädukten
ewiges Wasser in sie eingelenkt –:
das spiegelt jetzt und geht und glänzt in ihnen.

DER SCHWAN

Diese Mühsal, durch noch Ungetanes
    schwer und wie gebunden hinzugehn,
gleicht dem ungeschaffnen Gang des Schwanes.

Und das Sterben, dieses Nichtmehrfassen
jenes Grunds, auf dem wir täglich stehn,
seinem ängstlichen Sich-Niederlassen –:

in die Wasser, die ihn sanft empfangen
und die sich, wie glücklich und vergangen,
unter ihm zurückziehn, Flut um Flut;
während er unendlich still und sicher
immer mündiger und königlicher
und gelassener zu ziehn geruht.

Roman Sarcophagi

Why should we not choose to believe that we
(preoccupied with hatreds, with distress,
who must endure our own dividedness
and live in crass confusion timelessly)

are like a richly-carved sarcophagus
in which with all her rings and ribbons,
with at her side her glassware and the ikons,
in brittle cerements reduced to dust,

someone, something, had gradually decayed
until it disappeared into unseen,
unspeaking mouths. Could not some mind have made

a decent use of this…? Water!…to run
through culverts from the ancient aqueducts,
forever brimming in the thirsty stone.

The Swan

Like one who lives in drudgery, constrained
to plod through weary uncompleted toil,
the ungainly swan must labour overland.

And as when dying we anxiously depart
from all that once sustained us in this World,
he anxiously must quit dry land and cast

himself upon the waters, which receive him
as if contented and fulfilled to bear him;
prevailing over sequences of ripples
infinitely silent and secure
and all the time more regal, more assured,
casual in mastery he glides and sails.

KINDHEIT

Es wäre gut viel nachzudenken, um
von so Verlornem etwa auszusagen,
von jenen langen Kindheit-Nachmittagen,
die so nie wiederkamen – und warum?

Noch mahnt es uns –: vielleicht in einem Regnen,
aber wir wissen nicht mehr was das soll;
nie wieder war das Leben von Begegnen,
von Wiedersehn und Weitergehn so voll

wie damals, da uns nichts geschah als nur
was einem Ding geschieht und einem Tiere:
da lebten wir, wie Menschliches, das Ihre
und wurden bis zum Rande voll Figur.

Und wurden so vereinsamt wie ein Hirt
und so mit großen Fernen überladen
und wie von weit berufen und berührt
und langsam wie ein langer neuer Faden
in jene Bilder-Folgen eingeführt,
in welchen nun zu dauern uns verwirrt.

DER DICHTER

Du entfernst dich von mir, du Stunde.
Wunden schlägt mir dein Flügelschlag.
Allein: was soll ich mit meinem Munde?
mit meiner Nacht? mit meinem Tag?

Ich habe keine Geliebte, kein Haus,
keine Stelle auf der ich lebe.
Alle Dinge, an die ich mich gebe,
werden reich und geben mich aus.

Childhood

It would be good for us to ponder often
childhood's interminable afternoons –
remembering that whole world lost and gone.
Times pass – why can they not return?

For haunted memory safeguards them still,
perplexed we seek them in the falling rain;
our lives will never again appear as full
of meeting, recognition, moving on

as they were then, when we experienced
what things and beasts all know – no less, no more –
and lived like them but as humankind
our lives filled to the brim with metaphor.

Later we learned a shepherd's loneliness
and overburdened by immensity
and all the voices stirring, calling us,
each of us like a thread was gradually
woven into the endless tapestry
and learned to know confusion and distress.

The Poet

Fugitive moment! how fast you escape me:
how you can wound with each stroke of your wing!
All alone? then what was I given my tongue for;
why was I given these nights, or these days?

I have no particular place here,
no beloved, no house of my own.
Though I enrich every thing that I enter,
enriched, it will easily spend me again.

DIE SPITZE

Menschlichkeit: Namen schwankender Besitze,
noch unbestätigter Bestand von Glück:
ist das unmenschlich, daß zu dieser Spitze,
zu diesem kleinen dichten Spitzenstück
zwei Augen wurden? – Willst du sie zurück?

Du Langvergangene und schließlich Blinde,
ist deine Seligkeit in diesem Ding,
zu welcher hin, wie zwischen Stamm und Rinde,
dein großes Fühlen, kleinverwandelt, ging?

Durch einen Riß im Schicksal, eine Lücke
entzogst du deine Seele deiner Zeit;
und sie ist so in diesem lichten Stücke,
daß es mich lächeln macht vor Nützlichkeit.

II

Und wenn uns eines Tages dieses Tun
und was an uns geschieht gering erschiene
und uns so fremd, als ob es nicht verdiene,
daß wir so mühsam aus den Kinderschuhn
um seinetwillen wachsen –: Ob die Bahn
vergilbter Spitze, diese dichtgefügte
blumige Spitzenbahn, dann nicht genügte,
uns hier zu halten? Sieh: sie ward *getan*.

Ein Leben ward vielleicht verschmäht, wer weiß?
Ein Glück war da und wurde hingegeben,
und endlich wurde doch, um jeden Preis,
dies Ding daraus, nicht leichter als das Leben
und doch vollendet und so schön als sei's
nicht mehr zu früh, zu lächeln und zu schweben.

The Lacemaker

I

Humanity: a doubtful happiness,
its value not yet clear, still unassessed:
and is it human that this scrap of lace,
this tiny tightly-woven piece,
should cost two eyes? Should not that be redressed?

As trees disperse their essence through their rind,
did all your joy in life flow to this end?
You who are dead, who were deprived of light,
reduced in scale, does this contain your heart?

Fate left a loophole and your spirit fled
out through it and escaped from history –
for now this lace makes useful things absurd
and you live on in its fragility.

II

And if sometimes the work we labour at
and our achievements seem so mean, so small,
so far removed from us that we regret
that we exchanged our childhoods for such toil,
such hard endeavour – would not this piece of lace,
its floral pattern dense, a little yellowed,
be quite enough to keep us here, to hold us?
For, see! it was achieved: this thing was made.

Did life seem trivial to her, did she know
an urgency within herself, a joy,
and out of it this object had to grow
substantial, insubstantial as our destiny;
beauty as perfect as if made to show
a time had come to smile – a time to fly?

EIN FRAUEN-SCHICKSAL

So wie der König auf der Jagd ein Glas
ergreift, daraus zu trinken, irgendeines, –
und wie hernach der welcher es besaß
es fortstellt und verwahrt, als wär es keines:

so hob vielleicht das Schicksal, durstig auch,
bisweilen Eine an den Mund und trank,
die dann ein kleines Leben, viel zu bang
sie zu zerbrechen, abseits vom Gebrauch

hinstellte in die ängstliche Vitrine,
in welcher seine Kostbarkeiten sind
(oder die Dinge, die für kostbar gelten).

Da stand sie fremd wie eine Fortgeliehne
und wurde einfach alt und wurde blind
und war nicht kostbar und war niemals selten.

DIE GENESENDE

Wie ein Singen kommt und geht in Gassen
und sich nähert und sich wieder scheut,
flügelschlagend, manchmal fast zu fassen
und dann wieder weit hinausgestreut:

spielt mit der Genesenden das Leben;
während sie, geschwächt und ausgeruht,
unbeholfen, um sich hinzugeben,
eine ungewohnte Geste tut.

Und sie fühlt es beinah wie Verführung,
wenn die hartgewordne Hand, darin
Fieber waren woller Widersinn,
fernher, wie mit blühender Berührung,
zu liebkosen kommt ihr hartes Kinn.

A Woman's Fate

Out on a hunt a thirsty king might take
a glass from anybody there, to drink,
and ever afterwards its owner make
a treasure of the glass, thinking

it irreplaceable. So it occurs
occasionally to thirsty Fate to raise
a woman to its lips and drink from her.
But afterwards a life of commonplace,

anxious and mean, encloses her in glass
locked in a cabinet of rarities
(or of those things accounted valuable).

As if on lease, alien and out of place,
she must grow old and blind and valueless –
no longer precious; unexceptional.

The Convalescent

Just as a song will sound in narrow streets
closer at first, then seeming quite to fade
(as timid birds come nearly within reach
until, alarmed, they rise and fly away)

life teases her while she lies convalescing
and as she lies so weak and indolent,
feeling abandoned and self-pitying,
she makes an awkward movement with her hand.

She feels a strangeness, almost wickedness,
as the dry hand in which her fever burns
still filled with fever's weaknesses, illusions,
comes like a burning flower whose caress
touches her cheek and strokes its skin and bone.

DIE ERWACHSENE

Das alles stand auf ihr und war die Welt
und stand auf ihr mit allem, Angst und Gnade,
wie Bäume stehen, wachsend und gerade,
ganz Bild und bildlos wie die Bundeslade
und feierlich, wie auf ein Volk gestellt.

Und sie ertrug es; trug bis obenhin
das Fliegende, Entfliehende, Entfernte,
das Ungeheuere, noch Unerlernte
gelassen wie die Wasserträgerin
den vollen Krug. Bis mitten unterm Spiel,
verwandelnd und auf andres vorbereitend,
der erste weiße Schleier, leise gleitend,
über das aufgetane Antlitz fiel

fast undurchsichtig und sich nie mehr hebend
und irgendwie auf alle Fragen ihr
nur eine Antwort vage wiedergebend:
In dir, du Kindgewesene, in dir.

TANAGRA

Ein wenig gebrannter Erde,
wie von großer Sonne gebrannt.
Als wäre die Gebärde
einer Mädchenhand
auf einmal nicht mehr vergangen;
ohne nach etwas zu langen,
zu keinem Dinge hin
aus ihrem Gefühle führend,
nur an sich selber rührend
wie eine Hand ans Kinn.

Growing Up

This was her world. She had inherited
all that stood here as upright as a tree
and she endorsed its terror and its grace,
its images, abstractions, Ark and Covenant,
its pageants, as when nations celebrate.

She had accepted all and she had met
with flying things, with things that fled away,
with what was sinister or not-yet-known
and found it all as ordinary as one
who daily fetches water from the well.
Then in the midst of play this whole world changed
with nothing left as she'd remembered it
and silent, soft, white veils came floating down
to settle softly on her naked head...

She could not lift them and could scarcely see,
uncomprehendingly she heard a voice
which seemed to whisper, always to repeat:
You who were child – inside yourself, inside!

Tanagra

Fashioned in the shape
of a girl's hand, dead,
this small piece of clay
a hot sun might have fired
comes to life again
outlasting all desire,
nothing to reach out for
nothing it yearns to hold;
like a hand-propped head
self-engrossed, enclosed.

Wir heben und wir drehen
eine und eine Figur;
wir können fast verstehen
weshalb sie nicht vergehen, –
aber wir sollen nur
tiefer und wunderbarer
hängen an dem was war
und lächeln: ein wenig klarer
vielleicht als vor einem Jahr.

DIE ERBLINDENDE

Sie saß so wie die anderen beim Tee.
Mir war zuerst, als ob sie ihre Tasse
ein wenig anders als die andern fasse.
Sie lächelte einmal. Es tat fast weh.

Und als man schießlich sich erhob und sprach
und langsam und wie es der Zufall brachte
durch viele Zimmer ging (man sprach und lachte),
da sah ich sie. Sie ging den andern nach,

verhalten, so wie eine, welche gleich
wird singen müssen und vor vielen Leuten;
auf ihren hellen Augen die sich freuten
war Licht von außen wie auf einem Teich.

Sie folgte langsam und sie brauchte lang
als wäre etwas noch nicht überstiegen;
und doch: als ob, nach einem Übergang,
sie nicht mehr gehen würde, sondern fliegen.

Though we turn and ponder
amulet and urn
one after another
how can we discern
what it is that lasts?
Better to return
smiling and in wonder
to marvel at the past,
growing slightly wiser
as the years grow on?

Going Blind

She sat there like the others at their tea:
I noticed first the curious way she seemed
to hold her cup – a little anxiously.
It almost hurt when, once, she gave a smile.

And when finally everybody rose
amid the talk and laughter – as we strolled
informally between the various rooms
I noticed her once more. She followed still

yet she seemed set apart – tense as a singer
who must soon appear before
her audience. The smiling eyes,
two pools reflecting back the light, were clear.

It seemed a hindrance must be overcome
and once that was achieved, transfigured, she
whose progress was so slow, so wearisome,
need never walk again, for she would fly.

IN EINEM FREMDEN PARK
BORGEBY-GÅRD

Zwei Wege sinds. Sie führen keinen hin.
Doch manchmal, in Gedanken, läßt der eine
dich weitergehn. Es ist, als gingst du fehl;
aber auf einmal bist du im Rondel
alleingelassen wieder mit dem Steine
und wieder auf ihm lesend: Freiherrin
Brite Sophie – und wieder mit dem Finger
abfühlend die zerfallne Jahreszahl –.
Warum wird dieses Finden nicht geringer?

Was zögerst du ganz wie zum ersten Mal
erwartungsvoll auf diesem Ulmenplatz,
der feucht und dunkel ist und niebetreten?

Und was verlockt dich für ein Gegensatz,
etwas zu suchen in den sonnigen Beeten,
als wärs der Name eines Rosenstocks?

Was steht du oft? Was hören deine Ohren?
Und warum siehst du schließlich, wie verloren,
die Falter flimmern um den hohen Phlox.

ABSCHIED

Wie hab ich das gefühlt was Abschied heißt.
Wie weiß ichs noch: ein dunkles unverwundnes
grausames Etwas, das ein Schönverbundnes
noch einmal zeigt und hinhält und zerreißt.

Wie war ich ohne Wehr, dem zuzuschauen,
das, da es mich, mich rufend, gehen ließ,
zurückblieb, so als wärens alle Frauen
und dennoch klein und weiß und nichts als dies:

In a Foreign Park
Borgeby-gård

Though neither path leads anywhere at all,
     preoccupied in your reflections
and thinking you are lost, you might press on:
again you come upon the circle and the stone,
again your finger traces the inscription
Baroness Brite Sophie; just as before
you find the date is indecipherable
and it seems just as moving, though familiar.

What makes you linger for a second time
in this dark corner with its gloomy elms,
this sunless, damp and unfrequented grove?

And now what paradox could draw
you on to hunt in sunlit beds of flowers
as one might seek the label for a rose?

What makes you stand so still? What do you hear?
Why do you look so desolate and stare
at the tall phlox and swarming butterflies?

Parting

How long I've known what *parting* means, how well
     I know it still, invincible and cruel.
A dreadful thing, a thing which once more shows
what we hold dear, which it at once destroys.

How vulnerable I was, but then I learned
that those who cried to me yet let me go
would leave me all alone while they remained:
like shapes of women pale and far away

Ein Winken, schon nicht mehr auf mich bezogen,
ein leise Weiterwinkendes –, schon kaum
erklärbar mehr: vielleicht ein Pflaumenbaum,
von dem ein Kuckuck hastig abgeflogen.

TODES-ERFAHRUNG

Wir wissen nichts von diesem Hingehn, das
nicht mit uns teilt. Wir haben keinen Grund,
Bewunderung und Liebe oder Haß
dem Tod zu zeigen, den ein Maskenmund

tragischer Klage wunderlich entstellt.
Noch ist die Welt voll Rollen, die wir spielen.
Solang wir sorgen, ob wir auch gefielen,
spielt auch der Tod, obwohl er nicht gefällt.

Doch als du gingst, da brach in diese Bühne
ein Streifen Wirklichkeit durch jenen Spalt
durch den du hingingst: Grün wirklicher Grüne,
wirklicher Sonnenschein, wirklicher Wald.

Wir spielen weiter. Bang und schwer Erlerntes
hersagend und Gebärden dann und wann
aufhebend; aber dein von uns entferntes,
aus unserm Stück entrücktes Dasein kann

uns manchmal überkommen, wie ein Wissen
von jener Wirklichkeit sich niedersenkend,
so daß wir eine Weile hingerissen
das Leben spielen, nicht an Beifall denkend.

waving goodbyes no longer meant for me,
their gestures faint, no longer signifying,
mere objects in the distance, fluttering –
a cuckoo flying from a damson-tree.

Experience of Death

We know nothing of our departing, for
it refuses to confide in us.
Our wonder should not be required, nor
love nor hatred, faced with Death, whose

tragic mask of grief disfigures it.
The World is full of parts which we must play,
as long as we still wonder if we please
Death will perform its own unpleasing part.

But when you left us, a reality,
a ray of light, shone in upon our stage
through the same chink through which you'd slipped away:
real green, real sunshine on real foliage.

We still perform and anxiously recite
our hard-learned lines; from time to time we must
make actors' gestures. But your presence might,
though far from us, no longer in the cast,

descending like a breath of that reality
take hold of us sometimes and overcome us.
Then for a time we are transported: we
at last act *life* and look for no applause.

BLAUE HORTENSIE

So wie das letzte Grün in Farbentiegeln
sind diese Blätter, trocken, stumpf und rauh,
hinter den Blütendolden, die ein Blau
nicht auf sich tragen, nur von ferne spiegeln.

Sie spiegeln es verweint und ungenau,
als wollten sie es wiederum verlieren,
und wie in alten blauen Briefpapieren
ist Gelb in ihnen, Violett und Grau;

Verwaschnes wie an einer Kinderschürze,
Nichtmehrgetragnes, dem nichts mehr geschieht:
wie fühlt man eines kleinen Lebens Kürze.

Doch plötzlich scheint das Blau sich zu verneuen
in einer von den Dolden, und man sieht
ein rührend Blaues sich vor Grünem freuen.

VOR DEM SOMMERREGEN

Auf einmal ist aus allem Grün im Park
man weiß nicht was, ein Etwas, fortgenommen;
man fühlt ihn näher an die Fenster kommen
und schweigsam sein. Inständig nur und stark

ertönt aus dem Gehölz der Regenpfeifer,
man denkt an einen Hieronymus:
so sehr steigt irgend Einsamkeit und Eifer
aus dieser einen Stimme, die der Guß

erhören wird. Des Saales Wände sind
mit ihren Bildern von uns fortgetreten,
als dürften sie nicht hören, was wir sagen.

Es spiegeln die verblichenen Tapeten
das ungewisse Licht von Nachmittagen,
in denen man sich fürchtete als Kind.

Blue Hydrangea

A spoiled green paint left over in a jar
has coloured these dull leaves, so dried and wan
under the flowers that no longer own
a blue, but still reflect it from afar.

As if through tears, smudged and approximate,
faint as the blue of letters from the past
as if, perhaps, it would be better lost
decaying into yellows, greys and violet;

colours as washed-out as a pinafore
outworn, outgrown, discarded utterly,
showing how short the lives of children are.

But of a sudden blue seems born again
within one cluster: then, surprised, you see
a tender blue rejoice beside the green.

Before Summer Rain

All of a sudden, outside in the park,
something we cannot identify
has gone from all the green. Quietly
it presses closer to the windows; looks

inside. Then from the copse, urgent and clear
a plover calls. You think of Saint Jerome,
such weight of solitude and zeal is there
within this voice which cries out for the storm

to hear! As if they thought it quite forbidden
for them to overhear what might be said
the pictures and the walls themselves recede,

the faded tapestry palely returns
the fickle light of all those afternoons
when we as children learned to be afraid.

IM SAAL

Wie sind sie alle um uns, diese Herrn
in Kammerherrentrachten und Jabots,
wie eine Nacht um ihren Ordensstern
sich immer mehr verdunkelnd, rücksichtslos,
und diese Damen, zart, fragile, doch groß
von ihren Kleidern, eine Hand im Schooß,
klein wie ein Halsband für den Bologneser:
wie sind sie da um jeden: um den Leser,
um den Betrachter dieser Bibelots,
darunter manches ihnen noch gehört.

Sie lassen, voller Takt, uns ungestört
das Leben leben wie wir es begreifen
und wie sie's nicht verstehn. Sie wollten blühn,
und blühn ist schön sein; doch wir wollen reifen,
und das heißt dunkel sein und sich bemühn.

LETZTER ABEND
(AUS DEM BESITZE FRAU NONNAS)

Und Nacht und fernes Fahren; denn der Train
des ganzen Heeres zog am Park vorüber.
Er aber hob den Blick vom Clavecin
und spielte noch und sah zu ihr hinüber

beinah wie man in einen Spiegel schaut:
so sehr erfüllt von seinen jungen Zügen
und wissend, wie sie seine Trauer trügen,
schön und verführender bei jedem Laut.

Doch plötzlich wars, als ob sich das verwische:
sie stand wie mühsam in der Fensternische
und hielt des Herzens drängendes Geklopf.

Sein Spiel gab nach. Von draußen wehte Frische.
Und seltsam fremd stand auf dem Spiegeltische
der schwarze Tschako mit dem Totenkopf.

In the Drawing-Room

S o many gentlemen press round us, all
   wearing court-dress: white ruffles at the throat,
their Order's Star, all else as black as night,
inexorably growing darker still.
Delicate ladies too, puffed by their gowns,
upon each lap a little feminine hand
as a lapdog wears its slim collar-band,
are everywhere around us. They surround
the reader and the avid amateur
of bibelots – some still their property.

Considerate, they let us live as we
conceive a life – so different from their own
whose object was to flower, which must mean beauty.
But we desire ripeness, and that means
we must stay dark and strive assiduously.

The Last Evening

T he night; the distant thunder from the road
   as the long convoy rumbles past the park.
When his gaze lifted from the harpsichord
to turn to her, it was as one might look

into a glass and see himself reflected.
Her face held nothing but his own fresh face.
She saw his looks, so flattered by their sadness,
grow still more handsome with each note he played.

But then that faded suddenly. As if
to hold and quieten its pounding grief,
she pressed both hands against a heart too full.

Night's freshness drifted in. He ceased to play.
On the pier-table by the window lay
the tall black shako with the silver skull.

JUGEND-BILDNIS MEINES VATERS

Im Auge Traum. Die Stirn wie in Berührung
mit etwas Fernem. Um den Mund enorm
viel Jugend, ungelächelte Verführung,
und vor der vollen schmückenden Verschnürung
der schlanken adeligen Uniform
der Säbelkorb und beide Hände –, die
abwarten, ruhig, zu nichts hingedrängt.
Und nun fast nicht mehr sichtbar: als ob sie
zuerst, die Fernes greifenden, verschwänden.
Und alles andre mit sich selbst verhängt
und ausgelöscht als ob wirs nicht verständen
und tief aus seiner eignen Tiefe trüb –.

Du schnell vergehendes Daguerreotyp
in meinen langsamer vergehenden Händen.

SELBSTBILDNIS AUS DEM JAHRE 1906

Des alten lange adligen Geschlechtes
Feststehendes im Augenbogenbau.
Im Blicke noch der Kindheit Angst und Blau
und Demut da und dort, nicht eines Knechtes
doch eines Dienenden und einer Frau.
Der Mund als Mund gemacht, groß und genau,
nicht überredend, aber ein Gerechtes
Aussagendes. Die Stirne ohne Schlechtes
und gern im Schatten stiller Niederschau.

Das, als Zusammenhang, erst nur geahnt;
noch nie im Leiden oder im Gelingen
zusammgefaßt zu dauerndem Durchdringen,
doch so, als wäre mit zerstreuten Dingen
von fern ein Ernstes, Wirkliches geplant.

Portrait of My Father as a Young Man

Eyes full of dreams. A forehead that seems made
to ponder distances. His unsmiling mouth,
full-lipped and sensual, startling in its youth.
A trim dress-uniform enriched with braid.
The sabre's basket-hilt, held out in front,
supporting patient hands content to wait
and free from any urgency, inert:
yet they perhaps intend, growing so faint,
to grasp at distance and be first to die.
All else veiled in its own obscurity,
so indistinct I cannot understand
and deep within itself profoundly sad.

Old, dim daguerrotype, how fast you fade
between my own more-slowly-fading hands.

Self-Portrait, 1906

A steadfastness, his one inheritance
from old nobility, has stamped the brows,
but in the eyes still childhood's blue, its fears.
A waiter's or a woman's deference,
although not slavish, shows occasionally.
The mouth is large and what a mouth should be,
not too persuasive but quite eloquent
enough. A forehead still all innocence
prefers its own shade, stooped reflectively.

All is conjecture, none of it made whole,
neither by hardship nor by hard
endeavour knit into a work achieved:
but as if out of all these scattered parts
there was projected something true and real.

DER KÖNIG

Der König ist sechzehn Jahre alt.
Sechzehn Jahre und schon der Staat.
Er schaut, wie aus einem Hinterhalt,
vorbei an den Greisen vom Rat

in den Saal hinein und irgendwohin
und fühlt vielleicht nur dies:
an dem schmalen langen harten Kinn
die kalte Kette vom Vlies.

Das Todesurteil vor ihm bleibt
lang ohne Namenszug.
Und sie denken: wie er sich quält.

Sie wüßten, kennten sie ihn genug,
daß er nur langsam bis siebzig zählt
eh er es unterschreibt.

AUFERSTEHUNG

Der Graf vernimmt die Töne,
er sieht einen lichten Riß;
er weckt seine dreizehn Söhne
im Erb-Begräbnis.

Er grüßt seine beiden Frauen
ehrerbietig von weit –;
und alle, voll Vertrauen
stehn auf zur Ewigkeit

und warten nur noch auf Erich
und Ulriken Dorotheen,
die, sieben- und dreizehnjährig,
(sechzehnhundertzehn)
verstorben sind im Flandern,
um heute vor den andern
unbeirrt herzugehn.

90

The King

The King is sixteen years of age.
   Though only sixteen he is The State.
Like a trapped animal caged,
past privy-councillors' grey

heads he stares round the room everywhere.
Perhaps there is little he feels
except, when it brushes his jaw,
the cool golden chain of the Fleece.

The death-warrant still lies before him.
He looks at it but does not sign.
They believe that this touches him cruelly

but knowing him better would learn
that he counts up to seventy, slowly.
Then he pauses and then signs his name.

Reawakening

The Count hears Judgement sounding.
   Light shines through every fault
as he wakes thirteen sons
interred within their vault;

behind them, both his wives;
he greets them courteously
and all of them believers
they prepare for Eternity.

But they must wait for Erich
and Ulrike Dorothee,
who died so young in Flanders
in sixteen-hundred-and-ten
aged seven and thirteen
in order pure and sinless
to lead them all to Heaven.

DER FAHNENTRÄGER

Die Andern fühlen alles an sich rauh
und ohne Anteil: Eisen, Zeug und Leder.
Zwar manchmal schmeichelt eine weiche Feder,
doch sehr allein und lieblos ist ein jeder;
er aber trägt – als trüg er eine Frau –
die Fahne in dem feierlichen Kleide.

Dicht hinter ihm geht ihre schwere Seide,
die manchmal über seine Hände fließt.

Er kann allein, wenn er die Augen schließt,
ein Lächeln sehn: er darf sie nicht verlassen. –

Und wenn es kommt in blitzenden Kürassen
und nach ihr greift und ringt und will sie fassen –:

dann darf er sie abreißen von dem Stocke
als riß er sie aus ihrem Mädchentum,
um sie zu halten unterm Waffenrocke.

Und für die Andern ist das Mut und Ruhm.

DER LETZTE GRAF VON BREDERODE
ENTZIEHT SICH TÜRKISCHER GEFANGENSCHAFT

Sie folgten furchtbar; ihren bunten Tod
von ferne nach ihm werfend, während er
verloren floh, nichts weiter als: bedroht.
Die Ferne seiner Väter schien nicht mehr

für ihn zu gelten; denn um so zu fliehn,
genügt ein Tier vor Jägern. Bis der Fluß
aufrauschte nah und blitzend. Ein Entschluß
hob ihn samt seiner Not und machte ihn

The Standard-Bearer

Their uniform feels rough to them and mean:
  cold iron and sour leather and poor cloth
though sometimes there's the softness of a feather.
They feel unloved and they feel raw, uncouth.
Only he bears as if it were a woman
their standard in its brightly-coloured dress –
the heavy silk whose touch like a caress
brushes his hands and softly strokes his skin.
With eyes shut he can feel her smile within
but he, steadfast, must never let her go.

If *they* should come with breastplates all aglow
to struggle for her, to carry her away –
his duty is to tear her from the pole
as if to wrench her from virginity,
to guard her safe beneath his coat of mail.

And they all proudly share this chivalry.

The Last of the Counts of Brederode
Avoids Capture by the Turks

How furiously they pursued, and from afar
  hurled gaudy death towards him as he fled
and, helpless, stayed in range and rode in danger.
His noble pedigree no longer stood

for anything, for even animals
know how to flee before the hunt. But then
the river roared and gleamed, and resolution
gripped and delivered him from his distress

wieder zum Knaben fürstlichen Geblütes.
Ein Lächeln adeliger Frauen goß
noch einmal Süßigkeit in sein verfrühtes

vollendetes Gesicht. Er zwang sein Roß,
groß wie sein Herz zu gehn, sein blutdurchglühtes:
es trug ihn in den Strom wie in sein Schloß.

DIE KURTISANE

Venedigs Sonne wird in meinem Haar
ein Gold bereiten: aller Alchemie
erlauchten Ausgang. Meine Brauen, die
den Brücken gleichen, siehst du sie

hinführen ob der lautlosen Gefahr
der Augen, die ein heimlicher Verkehr
an die Kanäle schließt, so daß das Meer
in ihnen steigt und fällt und wechselt. Wer

mich einmal sah, beneidet meinen Hund,
weil sich auf ihm oft in zerstreuter Pause
die Hand, die nie an keiner Glut verkohlt,

die unverwundbare, geschmückt, erholt –.
Und Knaben, Hoffnungen aus altem Hause,
gehn wie an Gift an meinem Mund zugrund.

restoring him to his nobility.
Once more the mettle of the blood
of noble women, ancient family,

showed in the smile upon the doomed young face.
All heart, he spurred and leaped into the flood:
like a lord entering his castle gates.

The Courtesan

Venetian sunlight's finest metal
   burnishes my hair – the envy of
all alchemy. See how my eyebrows curve
and arch, like bridges safely spanned above

the thirsty waters of the grey canals
which are contracted to my fatal eyes
so that the sea forever ebbs and flows
and changes in their depths. Those

who once have looked at me will not forget
their envy of the dog on whom I let
my hand – invulnerable, exquisite,

and never scorched by flame – so often rest.
And young men fortunate in birth and gifts
find death, as though by poison, at my lips.

DIE TREPPE DER ORANGERIE

VERSAILLES

Wie Könige die schließlich nur noch schreiten
  fast ohne Ziel, nur um von Zeit zu Zeit
sich den Verneigenden auf beiden Seiten
zu zeigen in des Mantels Einsamkeit –:

so steigt, allein zwischen den Balustraden,
die sich verneigen schon seit Anbeginn,
die Treppe: langsam und von Gottes Gnaden
und auf den Himmel zu und nirgends hin;

als ob sie allen Folgenden befahl
zurückzubleiben, – so daß sie nicht wagen
von ferne nachzugehen; nicht einmal
die schwere Schleppe durfte einer tragen.

DER MARMOR-KARREN

PARIS

Auf Pferde, sieben ziehende, verteilt,
  verwandelt Niebewegtes sich in Schritte;
denn was hochmütig in des Marmors Mitte
an Alter, Widerstand und All verweilt,

das zeigt sich unter Menschen. Siehe, nicht
unkenntlich, unter irgendeinem Namen,
nein: wie der Held das Drängen in den Dramen
erst sichtbar macht und plötzlich unterbricht:

so kommt es durch den stauenden Verlauf
des Tages, kommt in seinem ganzen Staate,
als ob ein großer Triumphator nahte,

langsam zuletzt; und langsam vor ihm her
Gefangene, von seiner Schwere schwer.
Und naht noch immer und hält alles auf.

The Orangery Steps
Versailles

J ust as the ageing king might seem to stride,
  wearing the lonely, heavy, ermine gown,
  primarily to let himself be seen
by bowing courtiers on either side –

deliberately proceeding, by God's Grace,
the stairway rises up accompanied
by ever-deferential balustrades
and aims at Heaven but stays directionless:

it seems to warn subjects and servitors
to keep their distance, not to press too close;
and they remain too fearful to approach
or to take up the heavy train it wears.

The Marble-Wagon
Paris

S even great draught-horses take up the strain:
  the unmovable advances, pace by pace.
The marble's age and proud imperviousness
which brooded out of sight within the stone

are displayed openly among Mankind –
as in the theatre the Hero's role
within the moving plot must show it all
quite plain, halt it, then lead it to its end.

And as the day's sand gathers in the glass
it is as if the Triumph of an Emperor
with all its pomp and gravity drew near,

its figures of ceremony preceded by
the tired prisoners, walking heavily;
nearer and nearer, letting nothing pass.

BUDDHA

Schon von ferne fühlt der fremde scheue
Pilger, wie es golden von ihm träuft;
so als hätten Reiche voller Reue
ihre Heimlichkeiten aufgehäuft.

Aber näher kommend wird er irre
vor der Hoheit dieser Augenbraun:
denn das sind nicht ihre Trinkgeschirre
und die Ohrgehänge ihrer Fraun.

Wüßte einer denn zu sagen, welche
Dinge eingeschmolzen wurden, um
dieses Bild auf diesem Blumenkelche

aufzurichten: stummer, ruhiggelber
als ein goldenes und rundherum
auch den Raum berührend wie sich selber.

RÖMISCHE FONTÄNE
BORGHESE

Zwei Becken, eins das andre übersteigend
aus einem alten runden Marmorrand,
und aus dem oberen Wasser leis sich neigend
zum Wasser, welches unten wartend stand,

dem leise redenden entgegenschweigend
und heimlich, gleichsam in der hohlen Hand,
ihm Himmel hinter Grün und Dunkel zeigend
wie einen unbekannten Gegenstand;

sich selber ruhig in der schönen Schale
verbreitend ohne Heimweh, Kreis aus Kreis,
nur manchmal träumerisch und tropfenweis

sich niederlassend an den Moosbehängen
zum letzten Spiegel, der sein Becken leis
von unten lächeln macht mit Übergängen.

Buddha

Unprepared and from afar the traveller
    feels the golden radiance drifting from him
as if here in one place many kingdoms,
filled with remorse, had heaped their hidden treasure.

He stares amazed, as he approaches nearer,
at golden eyebrows, lofty and serene –
not at their ear-rings, ornaments of women,
or dishes, drinking-vessels, tableware.

Who can tell us of the things once melted
down to cast this image and to set it
upright within its calyx – like a flower

richer in stillness, softness, yellowness
than any thing of gold? And everywhere
fully in touch both with itself and Space.

Roman Fountain
Borghese

Flanked by a round, worn, ancient, marble rim,
    two basins: one, raised up above the other,
lets down its water gradually to brim
and join the water waiting in the lower –

which makes a silent answer to its murmur,
and shows it, cupped within its hollowed hand
as one might hold some curious object there,
a secret Heaven, green, obscure, profound;

spending itself without regret, content
to lap the ornate bowl, then spreading
out, ring following quietly on ring

it lets an absent-minded trickle go
sliding along the mossy ornaments –
the basin shining upwards at its flow.

99

DAS KARUSSELL
JARDIN DU LUXEMBOURG

Mit einem Dach und seinem Schatten dreht
sich eine kleine Weile der Bestand
von bunten Pferden, alle aus dem Land,
das lange zögert, eh es untergeht.
Zwar manche sind an Wagen angespannt,
doch alle haben Mut in ihren Mienen;
ein böser roter Löwe geht mit ihnen
und dann und wann ein weißer Elefant.

Sogar ein Hirsch ist da, ganz wie im Wald,
nur daß er einen Sattel trägt und drüber
ein kleines blaues Mädchen aufgeschnallt.

Und auf dem Löwen reitet weiß ein Junge
und hält sich mit der kleinen heißen Hand,
dieweil der Löwe Zähne zeigt und Zunge.

Und dann und wann ein weißer Elefant.

Und auf den Pferden kommen sie vorüber,
auch Mädchen, helle, diesem Pferdesprunge
fast schon entwachsen; mitten in dem Schwunge
schauen sie auf, irgendwohin, herüber –

Und dann und wann ein weißer Elefant.

Und das geht hin und eilt sich, daß es endet,
und kreist und dreht sich nur und hat kein Ziel.
Ein Rot, ein Grün, ein Grau vorbeigesendet,
ein kleines kaum begonnenes Profil –.
Und manchesmal ein Lächeln, hergewendet,
ein seliges, das blendet und verschwendet
an dieses atemlose blinde Spiel…

The Merry-Go-Round
Jardin du Luxembourg

The team of painted ponies spins around
   against the shadow of the canopy,
part of the ancient brightly-coloured land
which stays and clings and ends reluctantly;
and some draw little carriages behind
but all of them look mettlesome and strong.
A small white elephant goes sailing by,
the fierce red lion follows him along.
A stag as real as in some woodland scene
although it wears a saddle: on it rides
a tiny girl in blue, strapped safely in.

A small white elephant goes sailing by,
the lion bears a little boy in white,
the fearsome creature shows its teeth and glares,
the hot excited hands hold very tight.

And so they ride and so they circle round
and round again, and lively girls are there
for whom such games are practically outgrown
whose eyes look everywhere, search everywhere.

A small white elephant goes sailing by
and all continues hastening towards an end,
circling and circling round and finding none;
a red horse, and a green, a grey, and then
a little face, unfinished, just begun.

And sometimes children's voices unrestrained
sound out in brilliant laughter, while they stay
enchanted in their breathless, endless, play.

SPANISCHE TÄNZERIN

Wie in der Hand ein Schwefelzündholz, weiß,
eh es zur Flamme kommt, nach allen Seiten
zuckende Zungen streckt –: beginnt im Kreis
naher Beschauer hastig, hell und heiß
ihr runder Tanz sich zuckend auszubreiten.

Und plötzlich ist er Flamme, ganz und gar.

Mit einem Blick entzündet sie ihr Haar
und dreht auf einmal mit gewagter Kunst
ihr ganzes Kleid in diese Feuersbrunst,
aus welcher sich, wie Schlangen die erschrecken,
die nackten Arme wach und klappernd strecken.

Und dann: als würde ihr das Feuer knapp,
nimmt sie es ganz zusamm und wirft es ab
sehr herrisch, mit hochmütiger Gebärde
und schaut: da liegt es rasend auf der Erde
und flammt noch immer und ergiebt sich nicht –.
Doch sieghaft, sicher und mit einem süßen
grüßenden Lächeln hebt sie ihr Gesicht
und stampft es aus mit kleinen festen Füßen.

DER TURM

TOUR ST-NICOLAS, FURNES

Erd-Inneres. Als wäre dort, wohin
du blindlings steigst, erst Erdenoberfläche,
zu der du steigst im schrägen Bett der Bäche,
die langsam aus dem suchenden Gerinn

der Dunkelheit entsprungen sind, durch die
sich dein Gesicht, wie auferstehend, drängt
und die du plötzlich *siehst*, als fiele sie
aus diesem Abgrund, der dich überhängt

Spanish Dancer

A match is struck: the centre blazes white
before the flame spreads out in all directions
and, all around, the orange tongues ignite.
The audience in a circle. All at once
she comes alive and flares into her dance

and suddenly the dancer is all fire.

The eyes flash once: she sets ablaze her hair
then in an instant, boldly, brilliantly
whirls her whole dress alight – and you can see
two angry arms extended from the flames
like writhing serpents, rattling and alarmed.

At last it is enough, for she can spare
exactly this much fire, nothing more.
She rakes it up to cast it, roaring, down
and watches as it blazes on the ground
her manner masterful and arrogant.

Serene in victory she lifts her head
and smiling sweetly in acknowledgement
she stamps her sturdy feet and leaves it dead.

The Tower
Tour St-Nicolas, Furnes

Earth-centre. High above you lies
the world towards which you climb – the world of surface;
now, like a river underground, through darkness,
between steep banks as water seeks and flows,

you seek to resurrect yourself, still climbing,
ascending until all at once the depths
suspended over you in the abyss
directly overhead and all-enclosing

und den du, wie er riesig über dir
sich umstürzt in dem dämmernden Gestühle,
erkennst, erschreckt und fürchtend, im Gefühle:
o wenn er steigt, behangen wie ein Stier –:

Da aber nimmt dich aus der engen Endung
windiges Licht. Fast fliegend siehst du hier
die Himmel wieder, Blendung über Blendung,
und dort die Tiefen, wach und voll Verwendung,

und kleine Tage wie bei Patenier,
gleichzeitige, mit Stunde neben Stunde,
durch die die Brücken springen wie die Hunde,
dem hellen Wege immer auf der Spur,

den unbeholfne Häuser manchmal nur
verbergen, bis er ganz im Hintergrunde
beruhigt geht durch Buschwerk und Natur.

DER PLATZ
FURNES

Willkürlich von Gewesnem ausgeweitet:
von Wut und Aufruhr, von dem Kunterbunt
das die Verurteilten zu Tod begleitet,
von Buden, von der Jahrmarktstrufer Mund,
und von dem Herzog der vorüberreitet
und von dem Hochmut von Burgund,

(auf allen Seiten Hintergrund):

ladet der Platz zum Einzug seiner Weite
die fernen Fenster unaufhörlich ein,
während sich das Gefolge und Geleite
der Leere langsam an den Handelsreihn

show you the darkened timbers, massive framing:
it seems enormous, tilting threateningly,
releasing fears locked deep in memory;
hung like a great bull, hugely lumbering...

At last you feel the wind and see blue sky
and you are plucked out into gusty day
and all is light – it is as if you fly
above a land which waits expectantly

whose little scenes, pictured by Patenir,
show everything together, all hours at once,
and all the bridges leap and stride like hounds
pursuing along brightly-coloured ways

chasing the ribbon which the houses hide
until, bright in the distance, reassured,
it runs on through the leafy countryside.

The Town Square
Furnes

E nlarged in scale by all that it has seen
(the violence, tumult, and the ceremony
with which the sentenced went to execution),
through mouths of little shops which call – Come, buy!
and with the Duke on horseback riding in;
with all the wealth and pride of Burgundy,

surrounded on all sides by history

the market square tempts windows to draw near
and view its openness. And all the while
its busy space is parcelled out and shared
among the commerce of the rows of stalls

verteilt und ordnet. In die Giebel steigend,
wollen die kleinen Häuser alles sehn,
die Türme vor einander scheu verschweigend,
die immer maßlos hinter ihnen stehn.

QUAI DU ROSAIRE
BRÜGGE

Die Gassen haben einen sachten Gang
(wie manchmal Menschen gehen im Genesen
nachdenkend: was ist früher hier gewesen?)
und die an Plätze kommen, warten lang

auf eine andre, die mit einem Schritt
über das abendklare Wasser tritt,
darin, je mehr sich rings die Dinge mildern,
die eingehängte Welt von Spiegelbildern
so wirklich wird wie diese Dinge nie.

Verging nicht diese Stadt? Nun siehst du, wie
(nach einem unbegreiflichen Gesetz)
sie wach und deutlich wird im Umgestellten,
als wäre dort das Leben nicht so selten;
dort hängen jetzt die Gärten groß und gelten,
dort dreht sich plötzlich hinter schnell erhellten
Fenstern der Tanz in den Estaminets.

Und oben blieb? – Die Stille nur, ich glaube,
und kostet langsam und von nichts gedrängt
Beere um Beere aus der süßen Traube
des Glockenspiels, das in den Himmeln hängt.

and merchandise. From every gable
little houses stare with eager eyes.
Silent before each other stand the towers,
forever present and immeasurable.

Quai du Rosaire
Bruges

The little streets stroll at a gentle pace
   (dawdling like convalescents at a spa,
halting to wonder – what was it stood here?),
they take long rests each time they reach a *Place*

and wait; until another with one stride
as evening falls and detail starts to fade
leaps the canal which, silvered and fulfilled,
sustains a saturated, liquid world
of mirrored things that never were so real.

The town is almost lost. Now you can feel
(by some strange law of reciprocity)
its paradox awaking, firm and clear
as if it lived a life that was less rare,
as if it prized its gardens, hanging there,
while lighted windows suddenly declare
that dancers circle the *estaminets*.

And up above it all? Only the stillness
lingers in the air and takes its ease;
tasting the berries where its fancy falls
from the ripe bunches of the ringing bells.

BÉGUINAGE

BÉGUINAGE SAINTE-ELISABETH, BRÜGGE

I

Das hohe Tor scheint keine einzuhalten,
die Brücke geht gleich gerne hin und her,
und doch sind sicher alle in dem alten
offenen Ulmenhof und gehn nicht mehr
aus ihren Häusern, als auf jenem Streifen
zur Kirche hin, um besser zu begreifen
warum in ihnen so viel Liebe war.

Dort knieen sie, verdeckt mit reinem Leinen,
so gleich, als wäre nur das Bild der einen
tausendmal im Choral, der tief und klar
zu Spiegeln wird an den verteilten Pfeilern;
und ihre Stimmen gehn den immer steilern
Gesang hinan und werfen sich von dort,
wo es nicht weitergeht, vom letzten Wort,
den Engeln zu, die sie nicht wiedergeben.

Drum sind die unten, wenn sie sich erheben
und wenden, still. Drum reichen sie sich schweigend
mit einem Neigen, Zeigende zu zeigend
Empfangenden, geweihtes Wasser, das
die Stirnen kühl macht und die Munde blaß.

Und gehen dann, verhangen und verhalten,
auf jenem Streifen wieder überquer –
die Jungen ruhig, ungewiß die Alten
und eine Greisin, weilend, hinterher –
zu ihren Häusern, die sie schnell verschweigen
und die sich durch die Ulmen hin von Zeit
zu Zeit ein wenig reine Einsamkeit,
in einer kleinen Scheibe schimmernd, zeigen.

Béguinage
Béguinage Sainte-Elisabeth, Bruges

I

These tall gates do not seem to guard a prison,
 the bridge beyond will take you either way,
but none the less they live enclosed within
the garden with its elms and do not stray
except to walk along the narrow lane
which leads to church; for there they mean to learn
the reason for this love which grows in them.

There they kneel down disguised in spotless linen,
so much alike it seems one voice alone
is heard piercing and pure within the anthem –
but multiplied until it is a thousand
reflecting back from where the columns stand.
The voices scale the mountain, ever higher,
and on its summit fling themselves away
towards the heavens: there the angels seize them.

Then they rise quietly, remaining dumb
as with a nod they proffer holy water
(one signs the cross, and one receives it from her)
moist fingers touching foreheads leave them chilled
before they move to lips, so pale, so cold.

Then they return still chastely veiled, restrained
(the young nuns steady, older ones less certain,
and one old woman lagging far behind)
in silence back along the lane again.
The houses mutely swallow them all in
but sometimes in between the elms they pass
stark messages of utter loneliness
which shine within the narrow window-panes.

Was aber spiegelt mit den tausend Scheiben
das Kirchenfenster in den Hof hinein,
darin sich Schweigen, Schein und Widerschein
vermischen, trinken, trüben, übertreiben,
phantastisch alternd wie ein alter Wein?

Dort legt sich, keiner weiß von welcher Seite,
Außen auf Inneres und Ewigkeit
auf Immer-Hingehn, Weite über Weite,
erblindend, finster, unbenutzt, verbleit.

Dort bleibt, unter dem schwankenden Dekor
des Sommertags, das Graue alter Winter:
als stünde regungslos ein sanftgesinnter
langmütig lange Wartender dahinter
und eine weinend Wartende davor.

DIE MARIEN-PROZESSION
GENT

Aus allen Türmen stürzt sich, Fluß um Fluß,
hinwallendes Metall in solchen Massen
als sollte drunten in der Form der Gassen
ein blanker Tag erstehn aus Bronzeguß,

an dessen Rand, gehämmert und erhaben,
zu sehen ist der buntgebundne Zug
der leichten Mädchen und der neuen Knaben,
und wie er Wellen schlug und trieb und trug,
hinabgehalten von dem ungewissen
Gewicht der Fahnen und von Hindernissen
gehemmt, unsichtbar wie die Hand des Herrn;

und drüben plötzlich beinah mitgerissen
vom Aufstieg aufgescheuchter Räucherbecken,
die fliegend, alle sieben, wie im Schrecken
an ihren Silberketten zerrn.

II

W hat does the window of a thousand panes
project into the churchyard down below –
where deepest stillness, light and its reflections
are mingled, quenched, diminished, hugely grow
and age fantastically like vintage wine?

No-one knows how, but it is here that all
the outwardness and inwardness are one:
all the dimensions, timeless and ephemeral,
obscure and dazzling, pristine, overblown.

Yet grey of ancient winters still endures
behind this backcloth of bright summer's-day:
as if a man stood there attentively
behind it, waiting patiently:
as if a woman watched and wept before.

The Procession of the Virgin Mary
Ghent

F rom every tower blow following on blow
rings such a roar of metal that it sounds
as if, below them, with the streets as mould
the shining day were poured and cast in bronze,

and on its edge as decoration runs
the lively twining pattern, like a frieze,
of novice boys and slight and graceful maidens –
a stream whose movement breaks in waves and plays
beneath the banners' insubstantial weight
controlled by other forces, out of sight
but yet as potent as the hand of God;

the censers smoking – leaping up in flight
as if inciting everything to fly,
all seven together frantically
straining at silver chains, as if afraid.

111

Die Böschung Schauender umschließt die Schiene,
in der das alles stockt und rauscht und rollt:
das Kommende, das Chryselephantine,
aus dem sich zu Balkonen Baldachine
aufbäumen, schwankend im Behang von Gold.

Und sie erkennen über all dem Weißen,
getragen und im spanischen Gewand,
das alte Standbild mit dem kleinen heißen
Gesichte und dem Kinde auf der Hand
und knien hin, je mehr es naht und naht,
in seiner Krone ahnungslos veraltend
und immer noch das Segnen hölzern haltend
aus dem sich groß gebärdenden Brokat.

Da aber wie es an den Hingeknieten
vorüberkommt, die scheu von unten schaun,
da scheint es seinen Trägern zu gebieten
mit einem Hochziehn seiner Augenbraun,
hochmütig, ungehalten und bestimmt:
so daß sie staunen, stehn und überlegen
und schließlich zögernd gehn. Sie aber nimmt

in sich die Schritte dieses ganzen Stromes
und geht, allein, wie auf erkannten Wegen
dem Glockendonnern des großoffnen Domes
auf hundert Schultern frauenhaft entgegen.

DIE INSEL
NORDSEE

I

Die nächste Flut verwischt den Weg im Watt,
und alles wird auf allen Seiten gleich;
die kleine Insel draußen aber hat
die Augen zu; verwirrend kreist der Deich

The banks of onlookers define the bed
in which this river runs and roars and sways
and now, in ivory and gilded wood
they glimpse approaching what they all await,
its tents of gold brushing the balconies:

above a sea of white, they recognise
raised up on high in ancient Spanish clothes
the effigy with its small fervent face
and recognise the infant that it holds
and it comes closer to them, in its crown,
and kneeling there they see she has grown old;
the wooden hand above the cloth-of-gold
oblivious to age sends blessings down.

Now as she passes by those kneeling there
and as they shyly peer from down below
it seems as if she orders on her bearers:
her eyes blaze, fiercely unequivocal,
the eyebrows raised, haughty, imperious;
amazed they halt in wonder there awhile
and hesitate before continuing on.

Borne on the shoulders of the whole procession,
its footsteps hers, womanly, all alone,
she climbs once more the road to her cathedral,
towards the gaping doors, the thundering bells.

The Island in the North Sea

I

The tide wipes out the path across the flats,
   everything everywhere now looks alike.
The nearby island keeps its eyes tight shut.
Enclosing it on every side, the dyke

um ihre Wohner, die in einen Schlaf
geboren werden, drin sie viele Welten
verwechseln, schweigend; denn sie reden selten,
und jeder Satz ist wie ein Epitaph

für etwas Angeschwemmtes, Unbekanntes,
das unerklärt zu ihnen kommt und bleibt.
Und so ist alles was ihr Blick beschreibt

von Kindheit an: nicht auf sie Angewandtes,
zu Großes, Rücksichtsloses, Hergesandtes,
das ihre Einsamkeit noch übertreibt.

II

Als läge er in einem Krater-Kreise
auf einem Mond: ist jeder Hof umdämmt,
und drin die Gärten sind auf gleiche Weise
gekleidet und wie Waisen gleich gekämmt

von jenem Sturm, der sie so rauh erzieht
und tagelang sie bange macht mit Toden.
Dann sitzt man in den Häusern drin und sieht
in schiefen Spiegeln was auf den Kommoden

Seltsames steht. Und einer von den Söhnen
tritt abends vor die Tür und zieht ein Tönen
aus der Harmonika wie Weinen weich;

so hörte ers in einem fremden Hafen –.
Und draußen formt sich eines von den Schafen
ganz groß, fast drohend, auf dem Außendeich.

III

Nah ist nur Innres; alles andre fern.
Und dieses Innere gedrängt und täglich
mit allem überfüllt und ganz unsäglich.
Die Insel ist wie ein zu kleiner Stern

114

contains and stultifies the islanders,
born into sleep in which they will confuse
all worlds with one another. Words are sparse
and when they speak their only sentences

are like short epitaphs upon the weird
things, water-washed and unexplained,
which came to them and stayed. Objects like these

from childhood on are all that meets their eyes:
things inconsiderate, improvident,
which only underline their solitude.

II

As if it lay within a ring, a crater
of the moon, a dam surrounds each farm.
Their gardens, dressed alike, have wind-combed hair
like orphans roughly schooled by storm

and daily saddened by the deaths it brings.
The people keep indoors and stare for hours
at crooked mirrors showing exotic things
among familiar objects on their dressers.

At evening, someone's son might stroll outdoors
and draw some chords from his harmonica –
a wailing melody as soft as tears

he once heard playing in a foreign harbour.
Upon the outer dyke a sheep appears
larger than life and almost ominous.

III

What lives within is near. All else lies far
away. The things within, so busy, overfull
and everyday, stay inexpressible.
It is as if the island were a star

welchen der Raum nicht merkt und stumm zerstört
in seinem unbewußten Furchtbarsein,
so daß er, unerhellt und überhört,
allein

damit dies alles doch ein Ende nehme
dunkel auf einer selbsterfundnen Bahn
versucht zu gehen, blindlings, nicht im Plan
der Wandelsterne, Sonnen und Systeme.

HETÄREN-GRÄBER

In ihren langen Haaren liegen sie
mit braunen, tief in sich gegangenen Gesichtern.
Die Augen zu wie vor zu vieler Ferne.
Skelette, Munde, Blumen. In den Munden
die glatten Zähne wie ein Reise-Schachspiel
aus Elfenbein in Reihen aufgestellt.
Und Blumen, gelbe Perlen, schlanke Knochen,
Hände und Hemden, welkende Gewebe
über dem eingestürzten Herzen. Aber
dort unter jenen Ringen, Talismanen
aus augenblauen Steinen (Lieblings-Angedenken)
steht noch die stille Krypta des Geschlechtes,
bis an die Wölbung voll mit Blumenblättern.
Und wieder gelbe Perlen, weitverrolte, –
Schalen gebrannten Tones, deren Bug
ihr eignes Bild geziert hat, grüne Scherben
von Salben-Vasen, die wie Blumen duften,
und Formen kleiner Götter: Hausaltäre,
Hetärenhimmel mit entzückten Göttern.
Gesprengte Gürtel, flache Skarabäen,
kleine Figuren riesigen Geschlechtes,
ein Mund der lacht und Tanzende und Läufer,
goldene Fibeln, kleine Bogen ähnlich
zur Jagd auf Tier- und Vogelamulette,
und lange Nadeln, zieres Hausgeräte
und eine runde Scherbe roten Grundes,

too small and Space, fiercely dispassionate,
had crushed it unaware. It circles on
and unilluminated and unheard
proceeds alone

through darkness in an orbit of its own
intent on making end to all of this,
continuing blindly and outside the course
of galaxies, of other stars or suns.

Tombs of the Hetaerae

They lie in their long hair, with earth-brown faces.
  They have retreated deep into themselves;
eyes closed as if to spare them from more distances.
Their bones, their mouths, their flowers. Every mouth
has rows of even teeth, like travelling-chessmen
set in facing rows of ivory.
The flowers, the yellowed pearls, the slender hands;
the bones, the petticoats: the rotted web
which clothes the ruined heart. Below the rings
and amulets of blue-eyed lapis (lovers'
keepsakes) the silent crypt of sex
survives, brim-filled with flower-petals.
And yet more yellowed pearls, escaped, far-scattered,
and terracotta bowls, their sides adorned
with her own image, and shattered ointment-jars
whose greenish shards still keep their scent of flowers;
small figurines of gods, their household shrines:
hetaera-heaven, full of amorous gods!
Girdles forced open, scarabs, wafer-thin,
and little sculptures with huge phalluses;
a laughing mouth and dancers, athletes; gold
fibulae resembling tiny bows
to shoot at amulets of beasts or birds.
Long pins. Some ornate plates and crockery.
A rounded piece of potsherd; drawn
on its red ground, a four-horse-team

darauf, wie eines Eingangs schwarze Aufschrift,
die straffen Beine eines Viergespannes.
Und wieder Blumen, Perlen, die verrollt sind,
die hellen Lenden einer kleinen Leier,
und zwischen Schleiern, die gleich Nebeln fallen,
wie ausgekrochen aus des Schuhes Puppe:
des Fußgelenkes leichter Schmetterling.

So liegen sie mit Dingen angefüllt,
kostbaren Dingen, Steinen, Spielzeug, Hausrat,
zerschlagnem Tand (was alles in sie abfiel),
und dunkeln wie der Grund von einem Fluß.

Flußbetten waren sie,
darüber hin in kurzen schnellen Wellen
(die weiter wollten zu dem nächsten Leben)
die Leiber vieler Jünglinge sich stürzten
und in denen der Männer Ströme rauschten.
Und manchmal brachen Knaben aus den Bergen
der Kindheit, kamen zagen Falles nieder
und spielten mit den Dingen auf dem Grunde,
bis das Gefälle ihr Gefühl ergriff:

Dann füllten sie mit flachem klaren Wasser
die ganze Breite dieses breiten Weges
und trieben Wirbel an den tiefen Stellen;
und spiegelten zum ersten Mal die Ufer
und ferne Vogelrufe –, während hoch
die Sternenächte eines süßen Landes
in Himmel wuchsen, die sich nirgends schlossen.

ORPHEUS. EURYDIKE. HERMES

Das war der Seelen wunderliches Bergwerk.
Wie stille Silbererze gingen sie
als Adern durch sein Dunkel. Zwischen Wurzeln
entsprang das Blut, das fortgeht zu den Menschen,
und schwer wie Porphyr sah es aus im Dunkel.
Sonst war nichts Rotes.

whose trotting legs look like black lettering
(a number set to mark an entryway).
More flowers still, and still more scattered pearls,
a little lyre with bright-gilded horns,
and under gauzes like a fallen mist
an ankle-joint: a fragile butterfly,
emerging from the shoe, its chrysalis.

And so they lie replete with precious things:
with objects, trinkets, gemstones, household goods,
with broken toys (how full they were of things).
And they grow dark, dark as the river's bed.

For they *were* river-beds. Young men
had cast their frantic bodies down on them
(small waves, intent upon an after-life).
Grown men were rushing torrents. Sometimes boys
like timid streams came faltering from
their childhoods' hills to play
with what they found among the shallows, until
that steep descent seized all their consciousness.

Then they were filled with calm transparent waters
reaching from bank to bank across their breadth;
they moved in eddies in the deepest parts
and now at last returned the shimmering
reflections of their banks, echoes of birdsong.
Meanwhile, high over them, the starry nights
appropriate to a smiling countryside
grew huge and occupied the open sky.

Orpheus. Eurydice. Hermes

Here was the fabled silver-mine of souls.
They went as silently as any lode
of precious ore within that dark.
The heavy blood which flows in human veins
gleamed red as porphyry among the roots
but nothing else was red.

Felsen waren da
und wesenlose Wälder. Brücken über Leeres
und jener große graue blinde Teich,
der über seinem fernen Grunde hing
wie Regenhimmel über einer Landschaft.
Und zwischen Wiesen, sanft und voller Langmut,
erschien des einen Weges blasser Streifen,
wie eine lange Bleiche hingelegt.

Und dieses einen Weges kamen sie.

Voran der schlanke Mann im blauen Mantel,
der stumm und ungeduldig vor sich aussah.
Ohne zu kauen fraß sein Schritt den Weg
in großen Bissen; seine Hände hingen
schwer und verschlossen aus dem Fall der Falten
und wußten nicht mehr von der leichten Leier,
die in die Linke eingewachsen war
wie Rosenranken in den Ast des Ölbaums.
Und seine Sinne waren wie entzweit:
indes der Blick ihm wie ein Hund vorauslief,
umkehrte, kam und immer wieder weit
und wartend an der nächsten Wendung stand, –
blieb sein Gehör wie ein Geruch zurück.
Manchmal erschien es ihm als reichte es
bis an das Gehen jener beiden andern,
die folgen sollten diesen ganzen Aufstieg.
Dann wieder wars nur seines Steigens Nachklang
und seines Mantels Wind was hinter ihm war.
Er aber sagte sich, sie kämen doch;
sagte es laut und hörte sich verhallen.
Sie kämen doch, nur wärens zwei
die furchtbar leise gingen. Dürfte er
sich einmal wenden (wäre das Zurückschaun
nicht die Zersetzung dieses ganzen Werkes,
das erst vollbracht wird), müßte er sie sehen,
die beiden Leisen, die ihm schweigend nachgehn:

Rocks. Forest glades where nothing breathed.
Bridges to span the void. And, over there,
hung like a rain-cloud far above the ground,
the great, dead, blind, grey sheet
of lake soared far above its bed.
Only one path: a pale meandering thread
cast down upon the patient meadowland.

This was the road by which they came.

First the slight figure in the sky-blue cloak.
His footsteps bit great pieces from their way
and swallowed them down whole; his hot eyes stared
impatiently ahead; his heavy hands
hung down among the mantle's folds.
They had forgotten that the left hand held
the fragile lyre, engrafted to his arm
as climbing roses twine round olive boughs.
It was as if his senses had been split in two:
sight ran on ahead, then, like a dog
it wheeled and turned around
to stand expectant at the distant bend.
His hearing, like a scent, remained behind.
Sometimes he could believe it lingered
so far behind that he could hear the steps
of those two others who must follow him
through all this long ascent. But no, the sound
was his own footsteps echoing;
was no more than the wind stirred by his cloak.
He had to tell himself: *They follow still.*
He spoke the words aloud and heard them fade.
How soundlessly they moved! The silence gnawed
at him. Although he knew one backward glance
must utterly destroy the whole design
so nearly now achieved, he ached, he longed
at last to halt, to turn and look behind
and in the distance see those other two
who followed but who stayed so strangely mute:

Den Gott des Ganges und der weiten Botschaft,
die Reisehaube über hellen Augen,
den schlanken Stab hertragend vor dem Leibe
und flügelschlagend an den Fußgelenken;
und seiner linken Hand gegeben: *sie.*

Die So-geliebte, daß aus einer Leier
mehr Klage kam als je aus Klagefrauen;
daß eine Welt aus Klage ward, in der
alles noch einmal da war: Wald und Tal
und Weg und Ortschaft, Feld und Fluß und Tier;
und daß um diese Klage-Welt, ganz so
wie um die andre Erde, eine Sonne
und ein gestirnter stiller Himmel ging,
ein Klage-Himmel mit entstellten Sternen –:
Diese So-geliebte.

Sie aber ging an jenes Gottes Hand,
den Schritt beschränkt von langen Leichenbändern,
unsicher, sanft und ohne Ungeduld.
Sie war in sich, wie Eine hoher Hoffnung,
und dachte nicht des Mannes, der voranging,
und nicht des Weges, der ins Leben aufstieg.
Sie war in sich. Und ihr Gestorbensein
erfüllte sie wie Fülle.
Wie eine Frucht von Süßigkeit und Dunkel,
so war sie voll von ihrem großen Tode,
der also neu war, daß sie nichts begriff.

Sie war in einem neuen Mädchentum
und unberührbar; ihr Geschlecht war zu
wie eine junge Blume gegen Abend,
und ihre Hände waren der Vermählung
so sehr entwöhnt, daß selbst des leichten Gottes
unendlich leise, leitende Berührung
sie kränkte wie zu sehr Vertraulichkeit.

Sie war schon nicht mehr diese blonde Frau,
die in des Dichters Liedern manchmal anklang,
nicht mehr des breiten Bettes Duft und Eiland
und jenes Mannes Eigentum nicht mehr.

the God of distant journeys, God of Messages,
whose eyes were bright beneath the dusty hood,
his slender baton held in front of him
and at his feet the ever-beating wings;
beside him, held at his left hand, walked *she*.

This was the woman for the love of whom
more lamentation burst out from one lyre
than from the throats of all lamenting women
since the world began. Whose mourning
made a world – brought all things back again,
the forests, valleys, roads and villages;
their cattle, fields and streams; a world like ours
circled by sun and spanned by stars like ours –
but set quite differently within
those other heavens. So beloved was she.

She kept the God's left hand. Her gentle limbs
were still constrained by tatters of her shroud.
She followed patiently, uncertainly.
Like one whose time is near, all inwardness,
she did not see the figure far ahead
nor see the path which led them upward
towards the living world. All inwardness,
and fully-clothed in her own death, her treasure,
she had become like a sweet fruit of darkness:
she was all crammed with death
too huge and recent for her understanding.

She had acquired a new, inviolable
virginity: her sex had closed
as flowers close at evening;
her hands by now were so accustomed
to their widowhood that even the God's
ghostly and infinitely careful touch
gave her offence, as if too intimate.

No more was she the poet's golden Muse
whose note and essence sounded in his songs.
She was no longer his. She had been myrrh
and spices, his island in the marriage bed;

Sie war schon aufgelöst wie langes Haar
und hingegeben wie gefallner Regen
und ausgeteilt wie hundertfacher Vorrat.

Sie war schon Wurzel.

Und als plötzlich jäh
der Gott sie anhielt und mit Schmerz im Ausruf
die Worte sprach: Er hat sich umgewendet –,
begriff sie nichts und sagte leise: *Wer?*

Fern aber, dunkel vor dem klaren Ausgang,
stand irgend jemand, dessen Angesicht
nicht zu erkennen war. Er stand und sah,
wie auf dem Streifen eines Wiesenpfades
mit trauervollem Blick der Gott der Botschaft
sich schweigend wandte, der Gestalt zu folgen,
die schon zurückging dieses selben Weges,
den Schritt beschränkt von langen Leichenbändern,
unsicher, sanft und ohne Ungeduld.

ALKESTIS

Da plötzlich war der Bote unter ihnen,
hineingeworfen in das Überkochen
des Hochzeitsmahles wie ein neuer Zusatz.
Sie fühlten nicht, die Trinkenden, des Gottes
heimlichen Eintritt, welcher seine Gottheit
so an sich hielt wie einen nassen Mantel
und ihrer einer schien, der oder jener,
wie er so durchging. Aber plötzlich sah
mitten im Sprechen einer von den Gästen
den jungen Hausherrn oben an dem Tische
wie in die Höh gerissen, nicht mehr liegend,
und überall und mit dem ganzen Wesen
ein Fremdes spiegelnd, das ihn furchtbar ansprach.
Und gleich darauf, als klärte sich die Mischung,

she had become as fluent, sinuous, as hair;
she was as prodigal as fallen rain,
distributed like corn in famine.

She had become all root.

So that, when suddenly the God stopped short,
took both her hands in his and said
with pity in his voice: *He has looked back!*
she did not understand him, murmured: *Who?*

There in the distance, dark against
the sunlit world outside, a figure stood,
unrecognisable and indistinct.
And had to watch the Messenger,
the sorrowing God, turn back again
to follow her along that strip of pathway
over meadows, for already she
had started to walk back along that road,
her limbs constrained by tatters of her shroud,
her footsteps patient in uncertainty.

Alcestis

All of a sudden he, the messenger,
was present there among the seething crowd
tossed in their midst, one more ingredient,
an extra for the marriage feast. And they
were unaware of him, did not perceive
the presence of the God, stayed ignorant
of his divinity, which he held close
like a wet garment moulded to his skin.
He seemed like one of them, just any one
of those who came and went and passed among them.
But then one guest looked up, saw their young host
leap from the couch, appalled, his startled look
reflecting something frightful that addressed him.
The tumult died and all fell silent then,

war Stille; nur mit einem Satz am Boden
von trübem Lärm und einem Niederschlag
fallenden Lallens, schon verdorben riechend
nach dumpfem umgestandenen Gelächter.
Und da erkannten sie den schlanken Gott,
und wie er dastand, innerlich voll Sendung
und unerbittlich, – wußten sie es beinah.
Und doch, als es gesagt war, war es mehr
als alles Wissen, gar nicht zu begreifen.
Admet muß sterben. Wann? In dieser Stunde.

Der aber brach die Schale seines Schreckens
in Stücken ab und streckte seine Hände
heraus aus ihr, um mit dem Gott zu handeln.
Um Jahre, um ein einzig Jahr noch Jugend,
um Monate, um Wochen, um paar Tage,
ach, Tage nicht, um Nächte, nur um Eine,
um Eine Nacht, um diese nur: um die.
Der Gott verneinte, und da schrie er auf
und schrie's hinaus und hielt es nicht und schrie
wie seine Mutter aufschrie beim Gebären.

Und die trat zu ihm, eine alte Frau,
und auch der Vater kam, der alte Vater,
und beide standen, alt, veraltet, ratlos,
beim Schreienden, der plötzlich, wie noch nie
so nah, sie ansah, abbrach, schluckte, sagte:
Vater,
liegt dir denn viel daran an diesem Rest,
an diesem Satz, der dich beim Schlingen hindert?
Geh, gieß ihn weg. Und du, du alte Frau,
Matrone,
was tust du denn noch hier: du hast geboren.
Und beide hielt er sie wie Opfertiere
in Einem Griff. Auf einmal ließ er los
und stieß die Alten fort, voll Einfall, strahlend
und atemholend, rufend: Kreon, Kreon!
Und nichts als das; und nichts als diesen Namen.
Aber in seinem Antlitz stand das Andere,
das er nicht sagte, namenlos erwartend,
wie ers dem jungen Freunde, dem Geliebten,
erglühend hinhielt übern wirren Tisch.

but it was silence with a sediment
of low-pitched chatter and of frightened whispers,
the party stale and all its laughter spoiled.
At last they recognised the slender God
and saw how he stood there, impassive, full
of portent. They nearly knew it then
although when it was said it seemed too stark
for them to grasp, incomprehensible:
Admetus is to die. Within this hour.

At this the brittle shell which held his fear
cracked open, shattered; his hands flew out
in front of him, he bargained with the God
pleading with him for just a few years more,
for one, for one more year of youth,
for less than that, for months or even weeks,
and then for just some days – not even days,
for nights. For just this night. For this.
Which the cold God refused. Then he cried out
and losing all restraint shrieked out aloud,
cried out as did his mother when she bore him.
And she, his mother, then his father too,
approached and stood there, old and frail, perplexed
beside the weeping son who, all at once,
looked at them as he never had before,
was silent, swallowed, said: *Father, these few*
last crumbs of life, so dry they almost choke you,
cannot mean much – better to let them go!
You too, old woman, what should keep you here –
you, who have borne a child and lived your life?
He grasped them both together and he held
them there like beasts for sacrifice; and then
he thrust them from him suddenly and stood
and seemed to smile and seemed to breathe again.
Creon! he called, again he called: *Creon!*
Nothing but that, nothing except the name,
but his whole face showed what he did not say.
He shone with expectation as he sought
for the young man, for his beloved friend,
across the wreckage of the ruined feast.

127

Die Alten (stand da), siehst du, sind kein Loskauf,
sie sind verbraucht und schlecht und beinah wertlos,
du aber, du, in deiner ganzen Schönheit –

Da aber sah er seinen Freund nicht mehr.
Er blieb zurück, und das, was kam, war *sie*,
ein wenig kleiner fast als er sie kannte
und leicht und traurig in dem bleichen Brautkleid.
Die andern alle sind nur ihre Gasse,
durch die sie kommt und kommt –: (gleich wird sie da sein
in seinen Armen, die sich schmerzhaft auftun).

Doch wie er wartet, spricht sie; nicht zu ihm.
Sie spricht zum Gotte, und der Gott vernimmt sie,
und alle hörens gleichsam erst im Gotte:

Ersatz kann keiner für ihn sein. Ich *bins*.
Ich bin Ersatz. Denn keiner ist zu Ende
wie ich es bin. Was bleibt mir denn von dem
was ich hier war? Das *ists* ja, daß ich sterbe.
Hat sie dirs nicht gesagt, da sie dirs auftrug,
daß jenes Lager, das da drinnen wartet,
zur Unterwelt gehört: Ich nahm ja Abschied.
Abschied über Abschied.
Kein Sterbender nimmt mehr davon. Ich ging ja,
damit das Alles, unter Dem begraben
der jetzt mein Gatte ist, zergeht, sich auflöst –.
So führ mich hin: ich sterbe ja für ihn.

Und wie der Wind auf hoher See, der umspringt,
so trat der Gott fast wie zu einer Toten
und war auf einmal weit von ihrem Gatten,
dem er, versteckt in einem kleinen Zeichen,
die hundert Leben dieser Erde zuwarf.
Der stürzte taumelnd zu den beiden hin
und griff nach ihnen wie im Traum. Sie gingen
schon auf den Eingang zu, in dem die Frauen
verweint sich drängten. Aber einmal sah
er noch des Mädchens Antlitz, das sich wandte
mit einem Lächeln, hell wie eine Hoffnung,
die beinah ein Versprechen war: erwachsen

It stands to reason, he would say to him,
... how could these poor old people represent
a ransom for me? They are valueless!
While you yourself, so handsome and unspoiled...

But the dear friend was nowhere to be seen
among the guests – The one who came in answer
to his call was she, although her figure,
so slight, so vulnerable and so pale
in the white wedding-dress, seemed unfamiliar.
The others are the stones upon her path
which mark her way (closer and ever closer)
towards his arms, held out to her in pain.
He stands. He waits for her. But first she speaks.
Her words are not to him but to the God.
They can all hear her voice speak through the God:

No-one may ransom him but I.
I am his ransom, for no other life
has been pre-empted as is mine. What
now remains for me but this? This death is mine.
Did she not say, the One who sent you here?
Even the bed that waits for me within
belongs to death. I am prepared
and my farewells are said. All has been said:
what more can we take with us? It is my wish
to take upon myself and bear away
all that awaits my husband, in that world.
Take me there now. I mean to die for him.

It was as if she were already dead.
As swiftly as the wind will change at sea,
the God had turned and left her husband's side,
making a signal to him secretly
which set him free to live a hundred lives.
As one may fight and stumble in a dream
he groped towards them, but already they
had almost reached the entrance where a crowd
of women stood and wept. For the last time
she turned her shining face to him. She smiled

zurückzukommen aus dem tiefen Tode
zu ihm, dem Lebenden –

Da schlug er jäh
die Hände vors Gesicht, wie er so kniete,
um nichts zu sehen mehr nach diesem Lächeln.

GEBURT DER VENUS

An diesem Morgen nach der Nacht, die bang
vergangen war mit Rufen, Unruh, Aufruhr, –
brach alles Meer noch einmal auf und schrie.
Und als der Schrei sich langsam wieder schloß
und von der Himmel blassem Tag und Anfang
herabfiel in der stummen Fische Abgrund –:
gebar das Meer.

Von erster Sonne schimmerte der Haarschaum
der weiten Wogenscham, an deren Rand
das Mädchen aufstand, weiß, verwirrt und feucht.
So wie ein junges grünes Blatt sich rührt,
sich reckt und Eingerolltes langsam aufschlägt,
entfaltete ihr Leib sich in die Kühle
hinein und in den unberührten Frühwind.

Wie Monde stiegen klar die Kniee auf
und tauchten in der Schenkel Wolkenränder;
der Waden schmaler Schatten wich zurück,
die Füße spannten sich und wurden licht,
und die Gelenke lebten wie die Kehlen
von Trinkenden.

as if in hope, in promise to return,
to graduate from darkness and from death
come back again to him, the living one.

And so he knelt. He hid
his face inside his hands
to shut out from his eyes all but her smile.

The Birth of Venus

That morning when at last the dreadful night
all outcry, noise, unquietness, had passed
the seas broke open – cried out with one last cry.
And as that died away leaving behind
only a grey daybreak, a pale sky
subsiding to the fishes' silent depths,
the waves gave birth.

From the sea's sex below the shining curls
of foam that glisten in the early sun
the girl emerges drenched, confused and pale,
then as a leaf in bud uncurls and opens,
breaks out from its folds, her nakedness
tests and assents to the fresh morning breeze
rejoicing in this new and pristine World.

Like moons that rise and hide among the clouds
the bright knees merge into her shaded thighs;
the legs, still lost in shadow, tapering;
the shining of her supple feet displayed
and every muscle moving fluently
as when a thirsty throat moves, swallowing.

Und in dem Kelch des Beckens lag der Leib
wie eine junge Frucht in eines Kindes Hand.
In seines Nabels engem Becher war
das ganze Dunkel dieses hellen Lebens.
Darunter hob sich licht die kleine Welle
und floß beständig über nach den Lenden,
wo dann und wann ein stilles Rieseln war.
Durchschienen aber und noch ohne Schatten,
wie ein Bestand von Birken im April,
warm, leer und unverborgen, lag die Scham.

Jetzt stand der Schultern rege Waage schon
im Gleichgewichte auf dem graden Körper,
der aus dem Becken wie ein Springbrunn aufstieg
und zögernd in den langen Armen abfiel
und rascher in dem vollen Fall des Haars.

Dann ging sehr langsam das Gesicht vorbei:
aus dem verküzten Dunkel seiner Neigung
in klares, waagrechtes Erhobensein.
Und hinter ihm verschloß sich steil das Kinn.

Jetzt, da der Hals gestreckt war wie ein Strahl
und wie ein Blumenstiel, darin der Saft steigt,
streckten sich auch die Arme aus wie Hälse
von Schwänen, wenn sie nach dem Ufer suchen.

Dann kam in dieses Leibes dunkle Frühe
wie Morgenwind der erste Atemzug.
Im zartesten Geäst der Aderbäume
entstand ein Flüstern, und das Blut begann
zu rauschen über seinen tiefen Stellen.
Und dieser Wind wuchs an: nun warf er sich
mit allem Atem in die neuen Brüste
und füllte sie und drückte sich in sie, –
daß sie wie Segel, von der Ferne voll,
das leichte Mädchen nach dem Strande drängten.

So landete die Göttin.

An apple resting in a child's small hand
the tender belly cradled in her hips;
the only darkness her bright life would hold
contained within the navel's narrow cup;
then underneath a gentle wave arose
which ended where the thighs continued on
and like young birches standing in April
alone and sunlit, quite unshaded still,
her sex, alive and innocently shown.

And now the shoulders were a pair of scales
balanced upon the steady frame which rose
directly upwards like a fountain's jet,
then hung, uncertain, in the graceful arms
only, as streaming hair, again to fall
towards the basin of her waist and thighs.

Slowly the features of the downcast face
were gently raised up from their shaded plane
and, first, established shining and erect,
but soon abbreviated by the chin.
Straight as a sunbeam and as rigid as
the slender stalks which bear the sap to flowers
the slender arms reach out in front of her
like swans whose necks, outstretched, seek out their shore.

Her first breath came like the first winds at dawn
to fan the body further into life;
then in the branching tree of arteries
and veins, in all the fine capillaries
a whispering, as from deeply-buried springs
warm blood begins to sing. The wind,
freshening, inspires her timid breasts –
they fill with distance and she sails to shore
and now, at last, the Goddess reaches land.

Hinter ihr,
die rasch dahinschritt durch die jungen Ufer,
erhoben sich den ganzen Vormittag
die Blumen und die Halme, warm, verwirrt,
wie aus Umarmung. Und sie ging und lief.

Am Mittag aber, in der schwersten Stunde,
hob sich das Meer noch einmal auf und warf
einen Delphin an jene selbe Stelle.
Tot, rot und offen.

DIE ROSENSCHALE

Zornige sahst du flackern, sahst zwei Knaben
zu einem Etwas sich zusammenballen,
das Haß war und sich auf der Erde wälzte
wie ein von Bienen überfallnes Tier;
Schauspieler, aufgetürmte Übertreiber,
rasende Pferde, die zusammenbrachen,
den Blick wegwerfend, bläkend das Gebiß
als schälte sich der Schädel aus dem Maule.

Nun aber weißt du, wie sich das vergißt:
denn vor dir steht die volle Rosenschale,
die unvergeßlich ist und angefüllt
mit jenem Äußersten von Sein und Neigen,
Hinhalten, Niemals-Gebenkönnen, Dastehn,
das unser sein mag: Äußerstes auch uns.

Lautloses Leben, Aufgehn ohne Ende,
Raum-brauchen ohne Raum von jenem Raum
zu nehmen, den die Dinge rings verringern,
fast nicht Umrissen-sein wie Ausgepartes
und lauter Inneres, viel seltsam Zartes
und Sich-bescheinendes – bis an den Rand:
ist irgend etwas uns bekannt wie dies?
Und dann wie dies: daß ein Gefühl entsteht,
weil Blütenblätter Blütenblätter rühren?

Behind her, as light-footed she strolled
along that virgin coast, the morning filled
with flowers and sweet grasses, springing up –
disorderly and warm, as if disturbed at love.
She walked about her World and breathed and moved.

But then at noon upon the leaden hour
the sea rose up again: it threw
a dolphin's body on that very sand.
Wide open. Raw. Quite dead.

The Rose Bowl

You have watched anger blazing. Once you saw
two boys clenched in a single ball of rage
who rolled about the ground like maddened beasts
attacked by swarming bees, like actors over-
acting, steaming like foundering horses, eyeballs
rolling, baring their teeth as if to peel
the whole skull out through the snarling mouth.

But now you know how that may be forgotten.
Before you stands the bowl of roses, filled
unforgettably with what is most
extreme in tendency, extreme in essence;
all this is offered never to be given
and could be ours – reach even to ourselves.

A life of stillness, opening endlessly
and lived in space yet leaving unconsumed
that space which objects all the time diminish;
scarcely delineated, still unprinted,
so inward and so strangely soft and tender
so shining with a light that is its own:
do we know anything which is like this?
And then, that such sensations should be born
purely of petals touching other petals?

Und dies; daß eins sich aufschlägt wie ein Lid,
und drunter liegen lauter Augenlider,
geschlossene, als ob sie, zehnfach schlafend,
zu dämpfen hätten eines Innern Sehkraft.
Und dies vor allem: daß durch diese Blätter
das Licht hindurch muß. Aus den tausend Himmeln
filtern sie langsam jenen Tropfen Dunkel,
in dessen Feuerschein das wirre Bündel
der Staubgefäße sich erregt und aufbäumt.

Und die Bewegung in den Rosen, sieh:
Gebärden von so kleinem Ausschlagswinkel,
daß sie unsichtbar blieben, liefen ihre
Strahlen nicht auseinander in das Weltall.

Sieh jene weiße, die sich selig aufschlug
und dasteht in den großen offnen Blättern
wie eine Venus aufrecht in der Muschel;
und die errötende, die wie verwirrt
nach einer kühlen sich hinüberwendet,
und wie die kühle fühllos sich zurückzieht,
und wie die kalte steht, in sich gehüllt,
unter den offenen, die alles abtun.
Und *was* sie abtun, wie das leicht und schwer,
wie es ein Mantel, eine Last, ein Flügel
und eine Maske sein kann, je nach dem,
und *wie* sie's abtun: wie vor dem Geliebten.

Was können sie nicht sein: war jene gelbe,
die hohl und offen daliegt, nicht die Schale
von einer Frucht, darin dasselbe Gelb,
gesammelter, orangeröter, Saft war?
Und wars für diese schon zu viel, das Aufgehn,
weil an der Luft ihr namenloses Rosa
den bittern Nachgeschmack des Lila annahm?
Und die batistene, ist sie kein Kleid,
in dem noch zart und atemwarm das Hemd steckt,
mit dem zugleich es abgeworfen wurde
im Morgenschatten an dem alten Waldbad?

Or this, the manner of their opening:
one eyelid opens, underneath you find
a host of other eyelids tightly closed –
as if by tenfold sleep they would subdue
all that they see within. And then,
the light which penetrates through every petal:
they filter darkness from a thousand skies
which blazes fiercely to illuminate
the tangled stamens, bushy and erect.

Then – watch the roses, notice how they move,
their gestures are so minuscule
they would be imperceptible but that
the rays diverge and fill the universe.

Look at the white rose blithely opening
to stand revealed within its cup
like Venus rising naked from her shell;
then see this blushing one which helplessly
must reach across to touch the cooler one
although it shrinks away, withdrawing from it;
and see one colder still, clothed in itself,
below the others who, more generous,
shed everything – and see too what they shed:
it can be light or heavy, it can be
a cloak or else a burden, or a wing,
a mask for carnival, an anything –
undressing like a woman for her lover.

What might they not be? Was the yellow rose
now lying here discarded once the rind
around a fruit whose juice, a little stronger,
more vermilion, was this yellowness?
Was blossoming too much for this other one?
for in the air its pink-without-a-name
takes on an aftertaste of bitter violet.
And this, like cambric, is it not a dress
whose shift, as warm as breath, as delicate,
is still inside it? – taken off to bathe
in morning's shadows, at the woodland pool.

Und diese hier, opalnes Porzellan,
zerbrechlich, eine flache Chinatasse
und angefüllt mit kleinen hellen Faltern, –
und jene da, die nichts enthält als sich.

Und sind nicht alle so, nur sich enthaltend,
wenn Sich-enthalten heißt: die Welt da draußen
und Wind und Regen und Geduld des Frühlings
und Schuld und Unruh und vermummtes Schicksal
und Dunkelheit der abendlichen Erde
bis auf der Wolken Wandel, Flucht und Anflug,
bis auf den vagen Einfluß ferner Sterne
in eine Hand voll Innres zu verwandeln.

Nun liegt es sorglos in den offnen Rosen.

See this one, opal-tinted porcelain, as fragile
as a shallow china cup filled to the edge
with brightly-coloured little butterflies –
while this one contains nothing but itself.

Are they not all like this, all self-containing
if self-containing means they will transform
the world outside, the wind and rain, the patient
spring, the guilt, the unrest, muffled Destiny,
the darkness of the Earth at evening,
the wanderings, the migrations of the clouds,
and energies which drift from distant stars –
to change all to a handful of pure inwardness?

The roses hold all this, content, within them.

NEUE GEDICHTE II

A mon grand ami Auguste Rodin

ARCHAISCHER TORSO APOLLOS

Wir kannten nicht sein unerhörtes Haupt,
darin die Augenäpfel reiften. Aber
sein Torso glüht noch wie ein Kandelaber,
in dem sein Schauen, nur zurückgeschraubt,

sich hält und glänzt. Sonst könnte nicht der Bug
der Brust dich blenden, und im leisen Drehen
der Lenden könnte nicht ein Lächeln gehen
zu jener Mitte, die die Zeugung trug.

Sonst stünde dieser Stein entstellt und kurz
unter der Schultern durchsichtigem Sturz
und flimmerte nicht so wie Raubtierfelle;

und bräche nicht aus allen seinen Rändern
aus wie ein Stern: denn da ist keine Stelle,
die dich nicht sieht. Du mußt dein Leben ändern.

KRETISCHE ARTEMIS

Wind der Vorgebirge: war nicht ihre
Stirne wie ein lichter Gegenstand?
Glatter Gegenwind der leichten Tiere,
formtest du sie: ihr Gewand

bildend an die unbewußten Brüste
wie ein wechselvolles Vorgefühl?
Während sie, als ob sie alles wüßte,
auf das Fernste zu, geschürzt und kühl,

stürmte mit den Nymphen und den Hunden,
ihren Bogen probend, eingebunden
in den harten hohen Gurt;

manchmal nur aus fremden Siedelungen
angerufen und erzürnt bezwungen
von dem Schreien um Geburt.

Archaic Torso of Apollo

We never knew his legendary head
        nor saw the eyes set there like apples ripening.
But the bright torso, as a lamp turned low
still shines, still sees. For how else could the hard

contour of his breast so blind you? How could
a smile start in the turning thighs and settle
on the parts which made his progeny?
This marble otherwise would stand defaced

beneath the shoulders and their lucid fall;
and would not take the light
like panther-skin; and would not radiate

and would not break from all its surfaces
as does a star. There is no part of him
that does not see you. You must change your life.

Cretan Artemis

A breeze that blows down from the coastal hills:
        did not her brow gleam like some silver thing?
did you not fashion her out of the wind-
of-passage of swift animals?

moulding the tunic to her virgin breasts,
an intimation only, insubstantial,
while she, with nymphs and hounds, set off to test
her bow – quick, unencumbered, cool.

Into the farthest distance, racing on
as if all were familiar, all well known,
wearing her broad, stiff girdle like a girth –

sometimes her ears are angrily assailed
when cries from far-flung villages compel
her to be present: witness to a birth.

LEDA

Als ihn der Gott in seiner Not betrat,
erschrak er fast, den Schwan so schön zu finden;
er ließ sich ganz verwirrt in ihm verschwinden.
Schon aber trug ihn sein Betrug zur Tat,

bevor er noch des unerprobten Seins
Gefühle prüfte. Und die Aufgetane
erkannte schon den Kommenden im Schwane
und wußte schon: er bat um Eins,

das sie, verwirrt in ihrem Widerstand,
nicht mehr verbergen konnte. Er kam nieder
und halsend durch die immer schwächre Hand

ließ sich der Gott in die Geliebte los.
Dann erst empfand er glücklich sein Gefieder
und wurde wirklich Schwan in ihrem Schooß.

DELPHINE

Jene Wirklichen, die ihrem Gleichen
überall zu wachsen und zu wohnen
gaben, fühlten an verwandten Zeichen
Gleiche in den aufgelösten Reichen,
die der Gott, mit triefenden Tritonen,
überströmt bisweilen übersteigt;
denn da hatte sich das Tier gezeigt:
anders als die stumme, stumpfgemute
Zucht der Fische, Blut von ihrem Blute
und von fern dem Menschlichen geneigt.

Eine Schar kam, die sich überschlug,
froh, als fühlte sie die Fluten glänzend:
Warme, Zugetane, deren Zug
wie mit Zuversicht die Fahrt bekränzend,
leichtgebunden um den runden Bug

Leda

D riven to hide himself within the swan
whose beauty almost made him feel afraid
the lovesick God first faded – then was gone
from sight, his swanhood not yet tried.

Betrayed, she seeing him draw near
within the swan soon recognised the God
and could not fail to see what he desired.
Yet the deception had secured the deed:

when the God's proud white neck had forced away
her ever-weakening uncertain hand
he fell upon the maiden: frenziedly

he thrust into his love, dissolved in her.
Locked in her lap and every inch a swan
he felt a feather grow on every feather.

Dolphins

R ealists, they permitted similar creatures
space in the world to prosper and to dwell in,
seeing and recognising things familiar:
a kinship shared with creatures of the water
ruled by the God whose servants are the Tritons
spouting down deep, streaming up from the ocean.
They knew the creatures. They had always known
them different from the dull cold-natured fishes,
blood of their own warm blood and by degrees
related to the things they knew as human.

The manic shoals swim somersaulting by them,
trusting, companionable, in gay formation
wreathing around the bow as naturally
as ivy clothes the belly of an urn –
carefree, serene, secure from injury,

wie um einer Vase Rumpf und Rundung,
selig, sorglos, sicher vor Verwundung,
aufgerichtet, hingerissen, rauschend
und im Tauchen mit den Wellen tauschend
die Trireme heiter weitertrug.

Und der Schiffer nahm den neugewährten
Freund in seine einsame Gefahr
und ersann für ihn, für den Gefährten,
dankbar eine Welt und hielt für wahr,
daß er Töne liebte, Götter, Gärten
und das tiefe, stille Sternenjahr.

DIE INSEL DER SIRENEN

Wenn er denen, die ihm gastlich waren,
spät, nach ihrem Tage noch, da sie
fragten nach den Fahrten und Gefahren,
still berichtete: er wußte nie,

wie sie schrecken und mit welchem jähen
Wort sie wenden, daß sie so wie er
in dem blau gestillten Inselmeer
die Vergoldung jener Inseln sähen,

deren Anblick macht, daß die Gefahr
umschlägt; denn nun ist sie nicht im Tosen
und im Wüten, wo sie immer war.
Lautlos kommt sie über die Matrosen,

welche wissen, daß es dort auf jenen
goldnen Inseln manchmal singt –,
und sich blindlings in die Ruder lehnen,
wie umringt

von der Stille, die die ganze Weite
in sich hat und an die Ohren weht,
so als wäre ihre andre Seite
der Gesang, dem keiner widersteht.

buoyant, enchanted, through the hissing waters
they confidently greet the staring sailors –
diving and reappearing, ever changing
places with the waves, rising and falling
dancing around the trireme on its journey.

Grateful, the sailors took this creature, given
to share their lives of salt and lonely dangers,
imagining a world for their companion,
legends concerning him to tell for ever:
dolphins loved music, loved the gods, loved gardens,
the unfathomable silent cycles of the stars.

The Island of the Sirens

S ometimes late in the evening they would ask
   to hear the story of his voyages
and as they drank together in the dusk
he would recount his journeys and their dangers:

but how could words astonishingly show
their eyes what his had seen amazedly:
the islands of the archipelago
turning to gold, the glassy-calm blue sea?

For with this sight danger had been reversed,
their ship imperilled by no thundering shock
of elements, nothing so well-rehearsed:
they understood the silence of the rocks...

Of what lay there among those golden islands
awaiting them, each sailor was aware
and knew they were all lost if they should hear
its song. Like men inspired they leaned

into their oars, frantic to thrust their craft
far from the infinite stillness that surrounded
them, as if it were the counterpart
to that sweet song no mortal ear withstands.

KLAGE UM ANTINOUS

K einer begriff mir von euch den bithynischen Knaben
  (daß ihr den Strom anfaßtet und von ihm hübt…).
Ich verwöhnte ihn zwar. Und dennoch: wir haben
ihn nur mit Schwere erfüllt und für immer getrübt.

Wer vermag denn zu lieben? Wer kann es? – Noch keiner.
Und so hab ich unendliches Weh getan –.
Nun ist er am Nil der stillenden Götter einer,
und ich weiß kaum welcher und kann ihm nicht nahn.

Und ihr warfet ihn noch, Wahnsinnige, bis in die Sterne,
damit ich euch rufe und dränge: meint ihr den?
Was, ist er nicht einfach ein Toter. Er wäre es gerne.
Und vielleicht wäre ihm nichts geschehn.

DER TOD DER GELIEBTEN

E r wußte nur vom Tod was alle wissen:
  daß er uns nimmt und in das Stumme stößt.
Als aber sie, nicht von ihm fortgerissen,
nein, leis aus seinen Augen ausgelöst,

hinüberglitt zu unbekannten Schatten,
und als er fühlte, daß sie drüben nun
wie einen Mond ihr Mädchenlächeln hatten
und ihre Weise wohlzutun:

da wurden ihm die Toten so bekannt,
als wäre er durch sie mit einem jeden
ganz nah verwandt; er ließ die andern reden

und glaubte nicht und nannte jenes Land
das gutgelegene, das immersüße –.
Und tastete es ab für ihre Füße.

Lament for Antinoüs

None of you knew him at all, the Bithynian lad
  (none intervened in his fate, none delivered him from it).
Certainly I doted on him. I spoiled him: what of it?
We all laid our burdens upon him and left his life marred.

Who knows the secret of love? Anyone? No-one.
Endless calamity grew from my failure.
Now from among all the gods of the Nile, all its guardians,
I can no longer distinguish him, cannot draw near.

Why did you send him so far to the stars in the heavens?
Were you insane? Now I must press you and question:
Is it that one? Better for him to be dead; then
he might have escaped this. It need not have been.

Death of the Beloved

Of Death he knew what we know generally:
  Death takes us and it thrusts us into silence.
She was not torn from him, but silently
the sight of her was washed out from his eyes

till, gradually dissolved, she must have gone
gliding away into that unknown land
of Shades; there she would smile and shine upon
them like a maiden moon, forever kind.

And gradually the dead and he were kin
as if through her they had been close-related.
Although he heard the words the living said

he thought them false and paid them no attention:
Death's land, he thought, seemed kind and doubly sweet.
He read its braille for traces of her feet.

KLAGE UM JONATHAN

Ach sind auch Könige nicht von Bestand
und dürfen hingehn wie gemeine Dinge,
obwohl ihr Druck wie der der Siegelringe
sich widerbildet in das weiche Land.

Wie aber konntest du, so angefangen
mit deines Herzens Initial,
aufhören plötzlich: Wärme meiner Wangen.
O daß dich einer noch einmal
erzeugte, wenn sein Samen in ihm glänzt.

Irgend ein Fremder sollte dich zerstören,
und der dir innig war, ist nichts dabei
und muß sich halten und die Botschaft hören;
wie wunde Tiere auf den Lagern löhren,
möcht ich mich legen mit Geschrei:

denn da und da, an meinen scheusten Orten,
bist du mir ausgerissen wie das Haar,
das in den Achselhöhlen wächst und dorten,
wo ich ein Spiel für Frauen war,

bevor du meine dort verfitzten Sinne
aufsträhntest wie man einen Knaul entflicht;
da sah ich auf und wurde deiner inne: –
Jetzt aber gehst du mir aus dem Gesicht.

TRÖSTUNG DES ELIA

Er hatte das getan und dies, den Bund
wie jenen Altar wieder aufzubauen,
zu dem sein weitgeschleudertes Vertrauen
zurück als Feuer fiel von ferne, und
hatte er dann nicht Hunderte zerhauen,
weil sie ihm stanken mit dem Baal im Mund,
am Bache schlachtend bis ans Abendgrauen,

Lament for Jonathan

Are even Kings ephemeral?
And must they pass away like common things
while their impression, like a signet ring's,
continues to imprint the passive land?

Your life began with your own heart's initial,
but whose bright seed might bring you back alive?
My brother Jonathan, how could your light
so suddenly be finished...
Oh, who could beget you a second time?

And how could you be struck down by a stranger
while one who breathed as near to you as I
must stand and listen to the messenger,
must search for shelter like a wounded beast,
must bellow, lick the wound, must rage and cry?

For you are gone from me. For you were torn away
as one might tear the hair from tender places,
tear it from armpits, and from the groin,
tear from where women used to play

until you came: for you released my senses
and patiently untied their knotted skein
so that I lifted up my head and saw and loved you.
I shall not ever look on you again.

The Consolation of Elijah

He had achieved first one task then another
in order to rebuild the Covenant
as stone by stone he had repaired the altar
before his far-flung trust returned as fire;
had he not butchered hundreds, sword in hand,
their stench of Ba'al more than he could bear? –
beside the brook continuing the slaughter
until at last the evening-grey combined

das mit dem Regengrau sich groß verband.
Doch als ihn von der Königin der Bote
nach solchem Werktag antrat und bedrohte,
da lief er wie ein Irrer in das Land,

so lange bis er unterm Ginsterstrauche
wie weggeworfen aufbrach in Geschrei
das in der Wüste brüllte: Gott, gebrauche
mich länger nicht. Ich bin entzwei.

Doch grade da kam ihn der Engel ätzen
mit einer Speise, die er tief empfing,
so daß er lange dann an Weideplätzen
und Wassern immer zum Gebirge ging,

zu dem der Herr um seinetwillen kam:
Im Sturme nicht und nicht im Sich-Zerspalten
der Erde, der entlang in schweren Falten
ein leeres Feuer ging, fast wie aus Scham
über des Ungeheuren ausgeruhtes
Hinstürzen zu dem angekommnen Alten,
der ihn im sanften Sausen seines Blutes
erschreckt und zugedeckt vernahm.

SAUL UNTER DEN PROPHETEN

Meinst du denn, daß man sich sinken sieht?
Nein, der König schien sich noch erhaben,
da er seinen starken Harfenknaben
töten wollte bis ins zehnte Glied.

Erst da ihn der Geist auf solchen Wegen
überfiel und auseinanderriß,
sah er sich im Innern ohne Segen,
und sein Blut ging in der Finsternis
abergläubig dem Gericht entgegen.

152

majestically with the grey of rain
and that day's work was done.
The furious Queen sent threatening messages
that she would be avenged; like one insane

he fled into the desert till, exhausted,
he fell at last beneath a juniper
and howled out his despair: O hear me God
I am a broken thing! Use me no more!

At once an Angel came with food and water:
his strength returned to him, he was renewed
and travelled far through fields and over rivers
until he reached the mountains where the Lord

would visit him; and yet the Lord
was not within the tempest, nor in the rending
of the Earth, nor in the unconsuming,
heavy, turgid waves of flame
crawling along the ground as though in shame –
For the Unnameable came down, serene,
to greet the old man at his journey's end,
who in the gentle murmuring of his blood,
protected and yet awestruck, heard His name.

Is Saul Also among the Prophets?

Is any man aware of his decline?
No, for the King felt noble and secure
even while in rage he turned, intent to slaughter
the youth who played the harp, to end his line.

The evil spirit filled him with confusion
it overwhelmed and tore his soul apart.
Hungry for grace he sought it yet he found none
and there was darkness in his veins and heart,
no piety and only superstition.

Wenn sein Mund jetzt troff und prophezeite,
war es nur, damit der Flüchtling weit
flüchten könne. So war dieses zweite
Mal. Doch einst: er hatte prophezeit

fast als Kind, als ob ihm jede Ader
mündete in einen Mund aus Erz;
Alle schritten, doch er schritt gerader.
Alle schrieen, doch ihm schrie das Herz.

Und nun war er nichts als dieser Haufen
umgestürzter Würden, Last auf Last;
und sein Mund war wie der Mund der Traufen,
der die Güsse, die zusammenlaufen,
fallen läßt, eh er sie faßt.

SAMUELS ERSCHEINUNG VOR SAUL

Da schrie die Frau zu Endor auf: Ich sehe –
Der König packte sie am Arme: Wen?
Und da die Starrende beschrieb, noch ehe,
da war ihm schon, er hätte selbst gesehn:

Den, dessen Stimme ihn noch einmal traf:
Was störst du mich? Ich habe Schlaf.
Willst du, weil dir die Himmel fluchen
und weil der Herr sich vor dir schloß und schwieg,
in meinem Mund nach einem Siege suchen?
Soll ich dir meine Zähne einzeln sagen?
Ich habe nichts als sie...Es schwand. Da schrie
das Weib, die Hände vors Gesicht geschlagen,
als ob sie's sehen müßte: Unterlieg –

Und er, der in der Zeit, die ihm gelang,
das Volk wie ein Feldzeichen überragte,
fiel hin, bevor er noch zu klagen wagte:
so sicher war sein Untergang.

154

His mouth made sounds as though he prophesied
but all was counterfeit and only served
to gain time for the fugitive – for flight.
That was the second time. Yet once he lived,

when practically a child, as if all his blood
were at the service of a golden mouth –
where others' feet would walk his feet could stride,
he spoke his heart where others' mouths cried out.

Now nothing more remained but his great pile
of virtues overthrown all lying where they fell;
the golden mouth now no more than a gutter
which gathers up its rain, collecting water
until at last it voids and lets all spill.

Samuel Appears before Saul

Then the Witch of Endor cried: I see!
Grasping her arm the King demanded: Who?
And she described, still staring glassily,
what he expected – just as if he too

saw him who would no longer prophesy:
Why must you trouble me again,
drag me from sleep? The Heavens curse you
and the Lord is silent now and turns
away; in my old mouth do you seek victory?
Shall I number each tooth that still remains?
For there is nothing else, no prophecy.
As if she saw it all the woman hid
her eyes behind her hands, whispered: Submit!

He had been proud as King and had prevailed,
towering above his people like a banner:
he sank upon the ground and would not plead
for he knew now that his defeat was sure.

Die aber, die ihn wider Willen schlug,
hoffte, daß er sich faßte und vergäße;
und als sie hörte, daß er nie mehr äße,
ging sie hinaus und schlachtete und buk

und brachte ihn dazu, daß er sich setzte;
er saß wie einer, der zu viel vergißt:
alles was war, bis auf das Eine, Letzte.
Dann aß er wie ein Knecht zu Abend ißt.

EIN PROPHET

Ausgedehnt von riesigen Gesichten,
hell vom Feuerschein aus dem Verlauf
der Gerichte, die ihn nie vernichten, –
sind die Augen, schauend unter dichten
Brauen. Und in seinem Innern richten
sich schon wieder Worte auf,

nicht die seinen (denn was wären seine
und wie schonend wären sie vertan)
andre, harte: Eisenstücke, Steine,
die er schmelzen muß wie ein Vulkan,

um sie in dem Ausbruch seines Mundes
auszuwerfen, welcher flucht und flucht;
während seine Stirne, wie des Hundes
Stirne, *das* zu tragen sucht,

was der Herr von seiner Stirne nimmt:
Dieser, Dieser, den sie alle fänden,
folgten sie den großen Zeigehänden,
die Ihn weisen wie Er ist: ergrimmt.

The woman looked at him. She understood
she had destroyed a King. Seeing him starved
and anxious to restore him if she could,
she killed a calf and cooked it and baked bread,

prepared a meal for him and called him to it.
He sat there, only darkness in his heart,
empty at last of all except his fear.
Then, hungry as a labourer, he ate.

A Prophet

U nderneath the bushy eyebrows, eyes
  look out, dilated by the enormous sights
they have witnessed, bright with firelight
from the execution of the Statutes
which leave him alone inviolate.
And once more the words begin to rise

from within him – others, not his own
(what use *his* words, few and quietly-spoken?),
hard words, obdurate as lumps of iron
he must melt like a volcano, stones

bursting from his mouth in its eruption –
curses following on white-hot curses:
for his forehead like a faithful hound's
catches up, appropriates and wears

all his master casts from his own brows –
Him, the One whom they could also find
and could read His face, His pointing hands
and behold Him wrathful: furious.

JEREMIA

Einmal war ich weich wie früher Weizen,
doch, du Rasender, du hast vermocht,
mir das hingehaltne Herz zu reizen,
daß es jetzt wie eines Löwen kocht.

Welchen Mund hast du mir zugemutet,
damals, da ich fast ein Knabe war:
eine Wunde wurde er: nun blutet
aus ihm Unglücksjahr um Unglücksjahr.

Täglich tönte ich von neuen Nöten,
die du, Unersättlicher, ersannst,
und sie konnten mir den Mund nicht töten;
sieh du zu, wie du ihn stillen kannst,

wenn, die wir zerstoßen und zerstören,
erst verloren sind und fernverlaufen
und vergangen sind in der Gefahr:
denn dann will ich in den Trümmerhaufen
endlich meine Stimme wiederhören,
die von Anfang an ein Heulen war.

EINE SIBYLLE

Einst, vor Zeiten, nannte man sie alt.
Doch sie blieb und kam dieselbe Straße
täglich. Und man änderte die Maße,
und man zählte sie wie einen Wald

nach Jahrhunderten. Sie aber stand
jeden Abend auf derselben Stelle,
schwarz wie eine alte Citadelle
hoch und hohl und ausgebrannt;

Jeremiah

It was you who transformed the heart I offered
(I was still tender as the early wheat)
and in your rage with your fire it was fired
till now it rages like a lion-heart.

Then what a mouth it was that you required
of me when I was not more than a lad...
disaster on disaster, year on year,
poured out from it as from a wound unhealed.

Each day anew the sounds came forth from me
which, never satisfied, you had created
from this same mouth which nothing could destroy...
Is there a means by which it shall be muted

when finally the enemies we harried
and pursued are all defeated, when
all of them are scattered far and wide
and when the massacre has reached its end?

From that great heap of ruins shall again be heard
my voice unchanged, just as it always cried.

A Sibyl

They said she had been old an age ago.
Still she endured. They saw her every day
walk the same streets. Now they assessed her years
as foresters count trees – reckoning her

in terms of centuries. Still she survived
and every night they saw her standing there,
looking like some burnt castle's blackened tower,
a ruin where no-one any longer lived –

von den Worten, die sich unbewacht
wider ihren Willen in ihr mehrten,
immerfort umschrieen und umflogen,
während die schon wieder heimgekehrten
dunkel unter ihren Augenbogen
saßen, fertig für die Nacht.

ABSALOMS ABFALL

I

S ie hoben sie mit Geblitz:
der Sturm aus den Hörnern schwellte
seidene, breitgewellte
Fahnen. Der herrlich Erhellte
nahm im hochoffenen Zelte,
das jauchzendes Volk umstellte,
zehn Frauen in Besitz,

die (gewohnt an des alternden Fürsten
sparsame Nacht und Tat)
unter seinem Dürsten
wogten wie Sommersaat.

Dann trat er heraus zum Rate,
wie vermindert um nichts,
und jeder, der ihm nahte,
erblindete seines Lichts.

So zog er auch den Heeren
voran wie ein Stern dem Jahr;
über allen Speeren
wehte sein warmes Haar,
das der Helm nicht faßte,
und das er manchmal haßte,
weil es schwerer war
als seine reichsten Kleider.

160

defeated by the teeming brood of words
produced in her unbidden, uncontrolled:
some shrieked incessantly and flapped around,
others had flown their errands and returned –
crouched in the shadow of her eyebrows they prepared
for darkness, for the silent night to fall.

The Fall of Absolom

I

Bright trumpets blaze and shine
and blow their fanfares, roaring
to swell the banners filling
above the tent wide open,
the host of people cheering;
magnificent and golden,
he takes ten concubines! –

Accustomed to an ageing
protector's frugal deeds,
like wheatfields wind-blown, waving,
they prosper in his greed.

He hastens to a meeting,
so quick, so shining-bright
that all who see and hear him
stand dazzled by his light,

the light which leads his army
as starlight leads the years,
the golden head still burning
above the brazen spears –
No helmet fit to gather
that hot, abundant growth
of hair he sometimes hated
for its inordinate weight.

161

Der König hatte geboten,
daß man den Schönen schone.
Doch man sah ihn ohne
Helm an den bedrohten
Orten die ärgsten Knoten
zu roten Stücken von Toten
auseinanderhaun.
Dann wußte lange keiner
von ihm, bis plötzlich einer
schrie: Er hängt dort hinten
an den Terebinthen
mit hochgezogenen Braun.

Das war genug des Winks.
Joab, wie ein Jäger,
erspähte das Haar –: ein schräger
gedrehter Ast: da hings.
Er durchrannte den schlanken Kläger,
und seine Waffenträger
durchbohrten ihn rechts und links.

ESTHER

Die Dienerinnen kämmten sieben Tage
die Asche ihres Grams und ihrer Plage
Neige und Niederschlag aus ihrem Haar,
und trugen es und sonnten es im Freien
und speisten es mit reinen Spezereien
noch diesen Tag und den: dann aber war

die Zeit gekommen, da sie, ungeboten,
zu keiner Frist, wie eine von den Toten
den drohend offenen Palast betrat,
um gleich, gelegt auf ihre Kammerfrauen,
am Ende ihres Weges *Den* zu schauen,
an dem man stirbt, wenn man ihm naht.

A ll heard the King command them
to spare his handsome son.
Among desperate knots of men
they saw him, helmet gone,
hewing limbs to pieces
of red flesh, butchering them;
then he was seen by no-one
and still they battled on
till one, excited, spoke:
I see him – in that oak!
his scalp stretched like a drum!

All eyes turned to the sight.
Joab the ruthless hunter
espied the auburn hair
the branch from which he swayed.
He drove in both his spears
and ten grim armour-bearers
thrust home from left and right.

Esther

H er serving-women combed for seven days
the ashes of her grief and her distress,
the residue and lees of her misfortune,
out of her hair. They spread it in the sun.
For two days more they perfumed it with essences.
But now the time had come and when

without further delay, with no more choice
than one already dead, she stood upon
the steps of the forbidding palace
the doors stood open wide, awaiting her.
She leaned upon her maids – She saw the One
whom it was death to touch, to venture near.

Er glänzte so, daß sie die Kronrubine
aufflammen fühlte, die sie an sich trug;
sie füllte sich ganz rasch mit seiner Miene
wie ein Gefäß und war schon voll genug

und floß schon über von des Königs Macht,
bevor sie noch den dritten Saal durchschritt,
der sie mit seiner Wände Malachit
grün überlief. Sie hatte nicht gedacht,

so langen Gang zu tun mit allen Steinen,
die schwerer wurden von des Königs Scheinen
und kalt von ihrer Angst. Sie ging und ging –

Und als sie endlich, fast von nahe, ihn,
aufruhend auf dem Thron von Turmalin,
sich türmen sah, so wirklich wie ein Ding:

empfing die rechte von den Dienerinnen
die Schwindende und hielt sie zu dem Sitze.
Er rührte sie mit seines Szepters Spitze:
…und sie begriff es ohne Sinne, innen.

DER AUSSÄTZIGE KÖNIG

Da trat auf seiner Stirn der Aussatz aus
und stand auf einmal unter seiner Krone
als wär er König über allen Graus,
der in die Andern fuhr, die fassungsohne

hinstarrten nach dem furchtbaren Vollzug
an jenem, welcher, schmal wie ein Verschnürter,
erwartete, daß einer nach ihm schlug;
doch noch war keiner Manns genug:
als machte ihn nur immer unberührter
die neue Würde, die sich übertrug.

164

His brilliance fired the ruby that she wore
and made it blaze – She felt she was a jar
entirely filled with nothing but his power,
his countenance which overflowed her.
But now she had to cross another room
and still the antechamber lay between,
all malachite, oppressing her with green.
She had not thought to walk so far, to come
laden with all these jewels which all the time
absorbing the King's majesty grew heavier,
and colder too as they took up her fear.

Gradually she drew nearer. Now she saw
him, upright on his throne of tourmaline,
as potent as a tree or as a tower.
A servant by her side still steered her on
as weak with terror she began to swoon,
fell senseless to the ground before the King.
His sceptre touched her. She knew everything.

The Leper King

The leprosy showed plainly on his brow
and shone below the shining of the crown
as if he were the king of all affliction:
his fear spread out among them, all now

stared stupefied, appalled by this event:
like a bound prisoner, abject and constrained
he stood – like one awaiting execution
though none among them dared to strike him down:
he seemed inviolable, as if this meant
a gift, a virtue only now obtained.

LEGENDE VON DEN DREI LEBENDIGEN
UND DEN DREI TOTEN

Drei Herren hatten mit Falken gebeizt
und freuten sich auf das Gelag.
Da nahm sie der Greis in Beschlag
und führte. Die Reiter hielten gespreizt
vor dem dreifachen Sarkophag,

der ihnen dreimal entgegenstank,
in den Mund, in die Nase, ins Sehn;
und sie wußten es gleich: da lagen lang
drei Tote mitten im Untergang
und ließen sich gräßlich gehn.

Und sie hatten nur noch ihr Jägergehör
reinlich hinter dem Sturmbandlör;
doch da zischte der Alte sein:
– Sie gingen nicht durch das Nadelöhr
und gehen niemals – hinein.

Nun blieb ihnen noch ihr klares Getast,
das stark war vom Jagen und heiß;
doch das hatte ein Frost von hinten gefaßt
und trieb ihm Eis in den Schweiß.

DER KÖNIG VON MÜNSTER

Der König war geschoren;
nun ging ihm die Krone zu weit
und bog ein wenig die Ohren,
in die von Zeit zu Zeit

gehässiges Gelärme
aus Hungermäulern fand.
Er saß, von wegen der Wärme,
auf seiner rechten Hand,

166

The Legend of the Three Living
and the Three Dead Men

Three falconers, three hungry lords
    anxious to feast, rode home.
An old man led them through the wood
until their horses shied and reared
before the triple tomb.

A threefold stench offended
each nose and mouth and eye –
within, they could not doubt it,
three long-dead bodies lay
dissolving in decay.

Under the leather riding-hoods
the falconers' ears, still keen,
heard the words the old man whispered:
They could not pass through the needle's eye,
they cannot enter in.

Their falconers' hands stayed firm and warm,
their hearts beat fast from the chase,
but a cold blight followed the hunters home
and it chilled their sweat to ice.

The King of Münster

The King has met with justice.
    Clipped naked by its shears,
he finds the crown excessive
resting upon the ears

which must hear spiteful babble
resounding without end:
the hunger of the rabble.
He sits on his right hand

167

mürrisch und schwergesäßig.
Er fühlte sich nicht mehr echt:
der Herr in ihm war mäßig,
und der Beischlaf war schlecht.

TOTEN-TANZ

Sie brauchen kein Tanz-Orchester;
sie hören in sich ein Geheule
als wären sie Eulennester.
Ihr Ängsten näßt wie eine Beule,
und der Vorgeruch ihrer Fäule
ist noch ihr bester Geruch.

Sie fassen den Tänzer fester,
den rippenbetreßten Tänzer,
den Galan, den ächten Ergänzer
zu einem ganzen Paar.
Und er lockert der Ordensschwester
über dem Haar das Tuch;
sie tanzen ja unter Gleichen.
Und er zieht der wachslichtbleichen
leise die Lesezeichen
aus ihrem Stunden-Buch.

Bald wird ihnen allen zu heiß,
sie sind zu reich gekleidet;
beißender Schweiß verleidet
ihnen Stirne und Steiß
und Schauben und Hauben und Steine;
sie wünschen, sie wären nackt
wie ein Kind, ein Verrückter und Eine:
die tanzen noch immer im Takt.

to warm it, desolate.
The Lord in him is spent
and he feels counterfeit –
ashamed and impotent.

Danse Macabre

No need for dance-bands playing:
within them sounds a braying
and hooting and a screeching
like nests of hungry owls.
They smell of a decay
first faint but soon increasing.
They suppurate like boils.

They clasp the Dancer tightly
(his ribs embroidered over)
and with this gallant partner
they feel a perfect pair.
He dances nuns, he loosens
(for here they are all equal)
the coifs which bind their hair,
takes one pale as a taper
and plucks the slips of paper
which mark her Book of Prayer.

Soon all grow overheated
for they are richly clothed
in robes and hoods and jewels;
their heated rumps and brows
perspire, the sweat disgusts them;
sooner they would be naked
as infants or as fools
continuing, male and female,
to dance in perfect time.

DAS JÜNGSTE GERICHT

So erschrocken, wie sie nie erschraken,
ohne Ordnung, oft durchlocht und locker,
hocken sie in dem geborstnen Ocker
ihres Ackers, nicht von ihren Laken

abzubringen, die sie liebgewannen.
Aber Engel kommen an, um Öle
einzuträufeln in die trocknen Pfannen
und um jedem in die Achselhöhle

das zu legen, was er in dem Lärme
damals seines Lebens nicht entweihte;
denn dort hat es noch ein wenig Wärme,

daß es nicht des Herren Hand erkälte
oben, wenn er es aus jeder Seite
leise greift, zu fühlen, ob es gälte.

DIE VERSUCHUNG

Nein, es half nicht, daß er sich die scharfen
Stacheln einhieb in das geile Fleisch;
alle seine trächtigen Sinne warfen
unter kreißendem Gekreisch

Frühgeburten: schiefe, hingeschielte
kriechende und fliegende Gesichte,
Nichte, deren nur auf ihn erpichte
Bosheit sich verband und mit ihm spielte.

Und schon hatten seine Sinne Enkel;
denn das Pack war fruchtbar in der Nacht
und in immer bunterem Gesprenkel
hingehudelt und verhundertfacht.
Aus dem Ganzen ward ein Trank gemacht:
seine Hände griffen lauter Henkel,
und der Schatten schob sich auf wie Schenkel
warm und zu Umarmungen erwacht –.

170

The Last Judgement

Never did any know such fear, such terror.
Their limbs disjointed, some with bodies broken,
they cower in the graveyard burst asunder
in naked clods of earth, of clay, of ochre:

only their shrouds remain – they clutch them tight.
Suddenly there are Angels come to trickle
into the dry bone-sockets healing oils;
they halt at every corpse; under its armpit

they place some thing which throughout life's affray
each guarded lovingly and held in faith –
safely to keep it there and there to warm it:

that the hand of the Lord shall feel no discomfort,
assessing it, determining its worth,
descending from the heavens to judge and weigh.

The Temptation

In vain he drove into his flesh sharp thorns,
for his excited senses cried aloud
and screamed and were in labour and miscarried
giving birth to dreadful imps and demons,

misshapen faces, squinting, crawling, flying,
himself the only object and the focus
for all the mischief, the united malice,
of nullities who took him for their plaything.

His fecund senses bred more family
for in the night the monsters multiplied
a hundredfold, swarming more gaudily,
more botched, more speckled, even more distorted,
then melted and were liquid and were poured.
He seized the cups and drank them greedily.
The shadows opened like a pair of thighs
awakening to embrace him, warm and lewd.

Und da schrie er nach dem Engel, schrie:
Und der Engel kam in seinem Schein
und war da: und jagte sie
wieder in den Heiligen hinein,

daß er mit Geteufel und Getier
in sich weiterringe wie seit Jahren
und sich Gott, den lange noch nicht klaren,
innen aus dem Jäsen destillier.

DER ALCHIMIST

Seltsam verlächelnd schob der Laborant
den Kolben fort, der halbberuhigt rauchte.
Er wußte jetzt, was er noch brauchte,
damit der sehr erlauchte Gegenstand

da drin entstände. Zeiten brauchte er,
Jahrtausende für sich und diese Birne
in der es brodelte; im Hirn Gestirne
und im Bewußtsein mindestens das Meer.

Das Ungeheuere, das er gewollt,
er ließ es los in dieser Nacht. Es kehrte
zurück zu Gott und in sein altes Maß;

er aber, lallend wie ein Trunkenbold,
lag über dem Geheimfach und begehrte
den Brocken Gold, den er besaß.

And then he cried to call the Angel to him;
cried and the shining Angel came, was there
and like a huntsman whipped the demons, drove them
into the saint – to contain them once more

within himself as he had done for years
of wrestling with such bestiaries of evil,
in order from the ferment to distil
at last his God, so clouded, so unclear.

The Alchemist

With a strange smile he pushed the flask away
though it still fumed uneasily. He sensed
what was still lacking that was necessary
to fabricate the Noble Element:

a mind inspired by all the galaxies;
time and still more time, this above all,
thousands of years for his retorts to boil;
a consciousness as vast as all the seas.

Taking his vain obsession in his hands
he loosed it, let it fly into the night
back to propriety and back towards God.

Then, gloating, mumbling like a drunken man,
he crouched above the drawer which hid his secret:
the nugget of pure gold which he had made.

DER RELIQUIENSCHREIN

Draußen wartete auf alle Ringe
und auf jedes Kettenglied
Schicksal, das nicht ohne sie geschieht.
Drinnen waren sie nur Dinge, Dinge
die er schmiedete; denn vor dem Schmied
war sogar die Krone, die er bog,
nur ein Ding, ein zitterndes und eines
das er finster wie im Zorn erzog
zu dem Tragen eines reinen Steines.

Seine Augen wurden immer kälter
von dem kalten täglichen Getränk;
aber als der herrliche Behälter
(goldgetrieben, köstlich, vielkarätig)
fertig vor ihm stand, das Weihgeschenk,
daß darin ein kleines Handgelenk
fürder wohne, weiß und wundertätig:

blieb er ohne Ende auf den Knien,
hingeworfen, weinend, nichtmehr wagend,
seine Seele niederschlagend
vor dem ruhigen Rubin,
der ihn zu gewahren schien
und ihn, plötzlich um sein Dasein fragend,
ansah wie aus Dynastien.

DAS GOLD

Denk es wäre nicht: es hätte müssen
endlich in den Bergen sich gebären
und sich niederschlagen in den Flüssen
aus dem Wollen, aus dem Gären

ihres Willens; aus der Zwang-Idee,
daß ein Erz ist über allen Erzen.
Weithin warfen sie aus ihren Herzen
immer wieder Meroë

The Reliquary

Outside the smithy there was Destiny
waiting for links of chain and golden rings
(for she is powerless without such things);
inside it they were objects merely,
objects he wrought and made, even the crown
which black as anger he was working,
hammering it into a circlet, shaping
it to wear a flawless precious stone.

All the while his eyes grew colder, cold
as the well-water he drank each day.
When at last the exquisite reliquary
(priceless, sumptuous, wrought of finest gold)
stood before him waiting to contain
the sacred relic, the small white carpal bone
with its wonder-working history,

he sank to his knees and could not rise,
uncontrolled, unstrung, eyes full of tears,
casting down his very soul to pray
in the light of the unwinking ruby,
for it seemed to offer him protection
though it also called his life in question –
gazing like an eye that sees the dynasties.

Gold

Think of a time when it was not yet known;
still lay buried, brooding in the hills.
Then an inner urgency compelled
it to seek the rivers – seething down,

intent to prove itself the sovereign
metal, symbol of nobility.
Men obsessed with dreams of golden cities
built them in their hearts at first, but then

175

an den Rand der Lande, in den Äther,
über das Erfahrene hinaus;
und die Söhne brachten manchmal später
das Verheißene der Väter,
abgehärtet und verhehrt, nachhaus;

wo es anwuchs eine Zeit, um dann
fortzugehn von den an ihm Geschwächten,
die es niemals liebgewann.
Nur (so sagt man) in den letzten Nächten
steht es auf und sieht sie an.

DER STYLIT

Völker schlugen über ihm zusammen,
   die er küren durfte und verdammen;
und erratend, daß er sich verlor,
klomm er aus dem Volksgeruch mit klammen
Händen einen Säulenschaft empor,

der noch immer stieg und nichts mehr hob,
und begann, allein auf seiner Fläche,
ganz von vorne seine eigne Schwäche
zu vergleichen mit des Herren Lob;

und da war kein Ende: er verglich;
und der Andre wurde immer größer.
Und die Hirten, Ackerbauer, Flößer
sahn ihn klein und außer sich

immer mit dem ganzen Himmel reden,
eingeregnet manchmal, manchmal licht;
und sein Heulen stürzte sich auf jeden,
so als heulte er ihm ins Gesicht.
Doch er sah seit Jahren nicht,

set up Meröe throughout the world –
from earth's farthest edges to the skies
and in regions never yet disclosed.
Sons fulfilled their fathers' prophesies:
brought it home with them, debased and cold.

First it prospered, later turned away from
those it had already spoiled and weakened,
men whose affluence had done them harm.
In the night at the very end,
people say, it returns to haunt them.

The Stylite

Nations gathered, suffocating him,
for he could exalt them or condemn,
till he fled from his predicament,
quit the crowds of people and their stench
with numb hands to scale the lofty column

which stood there, now capped with emptiness,
and alone he perched on its summit
vigorously denouncing his own weakness
while he extolled the power of the Lord.

He preached on forever, he compared
and grew ever smaller by comparison
and the shepherds, farmers, watermen
watched his figure, much diminished, frenzied,

endlessly orating at the skies,
rain-soaked sometimes, sometimes under sun,
and his howling beat at everyone,
hammering against their naked faces.
At the end he had not known for years

wie der Menge Drängen und Verlauf
unten unaufhörlich sich ergänzte,
und das Blanke an den Fürsten glänzte
lange nicht so hoch hinauf.

Aber wenn er oben, fast verdammt
und von ihrem Widerstand zerschunden,
einsam mit verzweifeltem Geschreie
schüttelte die täglichen Dämonen:
fielen langsam auf die erste Reihe
schwer und ungeschickt aus seinen Wunden
große Würmer in die offnen Kronen
und vermehrten sich im Samt.

DIE ÄGYPTISCHE MARIA

S eit sie damals, bettheiß, als die Hure
übern Jordan floh und, wie ein Grab
gebend, stark und unvermischt das pure
Herz der Ewigkeit zu trinken gab,

wuchs ihr frühes Hingegebensein
unaufhaltsam an zu solcher Größe,
daß sie endlich, wie die ewige Blöße
Aller, aus vergilbtem Elfenbein

dalag in der dürren Haare Schelfe.
Und ein Löwe kreiste; und ein Alter
rief ihn winkend an, daß er ihm helfe:
(und so gruben sie zu zwein.)

Und der Alte neigte sie hinein.
Und der Löwe, wie ein Wappenhalter,
saß dabei und hielt den Stein.

all the thronging commerce of the crowds
swarming there so never-endingly
and the pomp and glitter of the lords
stayed invisible to one so high.

When, dismayed by their recalcitrance,
quite alone and almost quite defeated,
he lifted up his voice and cried aloud
shaking himself to rid himself of demons,
great white maggots dislodged from his wounds
fell on princely heads. In the velvet
linings of the open crowns
they nestled and they crawled and multiplied.

The Egyptian Mary

Hot from many beds, proclaimed a harlot,
she had fled long ago across the Jordan:
all-acceptant as the grave since then
she offered all her undiluted heart

as if she meant to slake eternity.
She grew from profligacy into greatness,
her spirit reaching out inexorably
till, finally, naked as human weakness
she lay there dead, her body yellowed ivory,
no longer glorious, the hair turned dross.

A lion circled her and an old man
following closely seemed to beckon to it.
Together man and lion scooped a pit;
when it was deep enough they laid her in,
the lion, heraldic, holding up the stone.

KREUZIGUNG

Längst geübt, zum kahlen Galgenplatze
irgend ein Gesindel hinzudrängen,
ließen sich die schweren Knechte hängen,
dann und wann nur eine große Fratze

kehrend nach den abgetanen Drein.
Aber oben war das schlechte Henkern
rasch getan; und nach dem Fertigsein
ließen sich die freien Männer schlenkern.

Bis der eine (fleckig wie ein Selcher)
sagte: Hauptmann, dieser hat geschrien.
Und der Hauptmann sah vom Pferde: Welcher?
und es war ihm selbst, er hätte ihn

den Elia rufen hören. Alle
waren zuzuschauen voller Lust,
und sie hielten, daß er nicht verfalle,
gierig ihm die ganze Essiggalle
an sein schwindendes Gehust.

Denn sie hofften noch ein ganzes Spiel
und vielleicht den kommenden Elia.
Aber hinten ferne schrie Maria,
und er selber brüllte und verfiel.

DER AUFERSTANDENE

Er vermochte niemals bis zuletzt
ihr zu weigern oder abzuneinen,
daß sie ihrer Liebe sich berühme;
und sie sank ans Kreuz in dem Kostüme
eines Schmerzes, welches ganz besetzt
war mit ihrer Liebe größten Steinen.

Crucifixion

Well used to driving various groups of wretches
to the stark Golgotha, the gallows-hill,
the soldiers loitered there a while.
From time to time they turned their heavy faces

incuriously towards the crucifixion
of the three. Meanwhile the clumsy butchery
was briskly dealt with and was swiftly done;
duty was over and the soldiers free.

Then one as spattered as a slaughterer
said to his Captain: That one just called out!
The officer rose in his saddle and looked over,
then reined his horse about for he too thought

that he had heard the voice, had heard it call:
Elijah! The soldiers gathered round beneath
the cross, proffering the sponge of vinegar and gall.
Lest he should die and disappoint them all
they wet the mouth that choked upon last breath.

They had believed more jests might yet be played.
They even thought: What if Elijah comes!
Below them in the distance Mary screamed
and once more he cried aloud and died.

Resurrection

He had not once denied her. He did not know
how to refuse to let her sing the praises of
their love and to lament her loss.
As a bird falls she fell beneath the cross,
a woman dressed from head to foot in sorrow
and wearing her most precious stones of love.

181

Aber da sie dann, um ihn zu salben,
an das Grab kam, Tränen im Gesicht,
war er auferstanden ihrethalben,
daß er seliger ihr sage: Nicht –

Sie begriff es erst in ihrer Höhle,
wie er ihr, gestärkt durch seinen Tod,
endlich das Erleichternde der Öle
und des Rührens Vorgefühl verbot,

um aus ihr die Liebende zu formen
die sich nicht mehr zum Geliebten neigt,
weil sie, hingerissen von enormen
Stürmen, seine Stimme übersteigt.

MAGNIFICAT

Sie kam den Hang herauf, schon schwer, fast ohne
an Trost zu glauben, Hoffnung oder Rat;
doch da die hohe tragende Matrone
ihr ernst und stolz entgegentrat

und alles wußte ohne ihr Vertrauen,
da war sie plötzlich an ihr ausgeruht;
vorsichtig hielten sich die vollen Frauen,
bis daß die junge sprach: Mir ist zumut,

als wär ich, Liebe, von nun an für immer.
Gott schüttet in der Reichen Eitelkeit
fast ohne hinzusehen ihren Schimmer;
doch sorgsam sucht er sich ein Frauenzimmer
und füllt sie an mit seiner fernsten Zeit.

Daß er mich fand. Bedenk nur; und Befehle
um meinetwillen gab von Stern zu Stern –.

Verherrliche und hebe, meine Seele,
so hoch du kannst: den HERRN.

And then she came, her face a mask of tears,
prepared to anoint him for his burial.
He stood and, resurrected, smiled at her
and for her own sake met her with denial.

The hollowness within her understood
how death had left him strengthened, why he scorned
her soothing oils and would not be anointed,
refused her grief and would not let her mourn:

he meant to build of her that loving woman
who keeps true faith but finds the strength to part;
whose courage and whose force surpasses all men's
when driven by the tempests of the heart.

Magnificat

Already large, she climbed the slope like one
no longer sure of counsel, hope or aid.
Then, meeting with that stately pregnant matron
who came towards her gravely with such pride

and seemed to know all that she would not tell
she felt herself restored by her and heartened.
Both of them heavy, they embraced, both careful,
and then the younger spoke: Dear friend

I feel as if chosen to live for ever
for God almost averts his eyes to pour
the glitter into rich men's vanities
yet he seeks out one woman with tender care
and takes and fills her with eternity,

and it was I he found, only consider,
on *my* account commandments spanned the stars!

My soul! you must forever praise
and magnify the Lord your God forever.

183

ADAM

S taunend steht er an der Kathedrale
steilem Aufstieg, nah der Fensterrose,
wie erschreckt von der Apotheose,
welche wuchs und ihn mit einem Male

niederstellte über die und die.
Und er ragt und freut sich seiner Dauer
schlicht entschlossen; als der Ackerbauer
der begann, und der nicht wußte, wie

aus dem fertig-vollen Garten Eden
einen Ausweg in die neue Erde
finden. Gott war schwer zu überreden;

und er drohte ihm, statt zu gewähren,
immer wieder, daß er sterben werde.
Doch der Mensch bestand: sie wird gebären.

EVA

E infach steht sie an der Kathedrale
großem Aufstieg, nah der Fensterrose,
mit dem Apfel in der Apfelpose,
schuldlos-schuldig ein für alle Male

an dem Wachsenden, das sie gebar,
seit sie aus dem Kreis der Ewigkeiten
liebend fortging, um sich durchzustreiten
durch die Erde, wie ein junges Jahr.

Ach, sie hätte gern in jenem Land
noch ein wenig weilen mögen, achtend
auf der Tiere Eintracht und Verstand.

Doch da sie den Mann entschlossen fand,
ging sie mit ihm, nach dem Tode trachtend;
und sie hatte Gott noch kaum gekannt.

184

Adam

High on the elevation near the rose-
window of the great cathedral he
stands in wonder, so peremptorily
set down, so like a god, above all creatures,

over these and those. And he rose up,
confident in his strength, and joyfully
resolved to husband and to till the soil,
although unsure of how they might escape

from Paradise, where all was ready-made,
instead to make their home on this new Earth.
He found his God not easy to persuade

and he was warned by Him, for he was told
repeatedly that this must bring him death.
But Man rejoined: Not so, for *she* is birth.

Eve

Carved on the elevation near the rose-
window of the great cathedral, she
now and forever stands, artlessly
holding the apple, in the apple-pose,

innocent, guilty of what grew to birth
after she went away, when lovingly
she left the cycles of eternity
like a tender Spring to strive on Earth.

She would have liked to linger there a while
studying gradually to acquire
the wisdom and accord of animals.

But since she saw that he was quite resolved,
intent on death, she kept him company,
although as yet she scarcely knew his God.

185

IRRE IM GARTEN
DIJON

Noch schließt die aufgegebene Kartause
sich um den Hof, als würde etwas heil.
Auch die sie jetzt bewohnen, haben Pause
und nehmen nicht am Leben draußen teil.

Was irgend kommen konnte, das verlief.
Nun gehn sie gerne mit bekannten Wegen,
und trennen sich und kommen sich entgegen,
als ob sie kreisten, willig, primitiv.

Zwar manche pflegen dort die Frühlingsbeete,
demütig, dürftig, hingekniet;
aber sie haben, wenn es keiner sieht,
eine verheimlichte, verdrehte

Gebärde für das zarte frühe Gras,
ein prüfendes, verschüchtertes Liebkosen:
denn das ist freundlich, und das Rot der Rosen
wird vielleicht drohend sein und Übermaß

und wird veilleicht schon wieder übersteigen,
was ihre Seele wiederkennt und weiß.
Dies aber läßt sich noch verschweigen:
wie gut das Gras ist und wie leis.

DIE IRREN

Und sie schweigen, weil die Scheidewände
weggenommen sind aus ihrem Sinn,
und die Stunden, da man sie verstände,
heben an und gehen hin.

The Asylum Garden
Dijon

The building which was once a Charterhouse
   still binds its courtyard as you bind a wound
and still its people live in it enclosed;
safe from a world they do not comprehend.

What might have been a life has passed them by.
They pass by one another. They return.
They move in circles. Simple and compliant
they walk along the long-familiar ways.

Some of them crouch to tend the early flowers.
Humble and self-effacing on their knees
they conduct secretly, when no-one sees,
a private and eccentric love-affair:

they woo the pale-green blades of tender grass
which shyly, tentatively, they caress.
It seems so innocent, unlike the roses
whose bright red, too like anger, seems excess

and threatens that it might well over-run
what their own hearts can hold and understand.
For even they possess something unspoken:
the gentleness of grass, that grass stays kind.

Madness

They keep their silence, for the walls that should
   contain their thoughts and hold them separate
are down. Like clocks whose time slips by untold –
wound up to strike but still remaining mute.

Nächtens oft, wenn sie ans Fenster treten:
plötzlich ist es alles gut.
Ihre Hände liegen im Konkreten,
und das Herz ist hoch und könnte beten,
und die Augen schauen ausgeruht

auf den unverhofften, oftenstellten
Garten im beruhigten Geviert,
der im Widerschein der fremden Welten
weiterwächst und niemals sich verliert.

AUS DEM LEBEN EINES HEILIGEN

Er kannte Ängste, deren Eingang schon
wie Sterben war und nicht zu überstehen.
Sein Herz erlernte, langsam durchzugehen;
er zog es groß wie einen Sohn.
Und namenlose Nöte kannte er,
finster und ohne Morgen wie Verschläge;
und seine Seele gab er folgsam her,
da sie erwachsen war, auf daß sie läge

bei ihrem Bräutigam und Herrn; und blieb
allein zurück an einem solchen Orte,
wo das Alleinsein alles übertrieb,
und wohnte weit und wollte niemals Worte.

Aber dafür, nach Zeit und Zeit, erfuhr
er auch das Glück, sich in die eignen Hände,
damit er eine Zärtlichkeit empfände,
zu legen wie die ganze Kreatur.

Sometimes at night they stand beside the window
and all at once it changes: all is well.
Their grateful hearts give thanks the world is real.
Reality lies all around their hands.
As if refreshed, made new, their eyes now dwell

on what had been so nightmarish, so changed:
the peaceful garden in the rational square
within the world from which they were estranged
is green forever, not to disappear.

From the Life of a Saint

He knew such terror that its overture,
like death, was not to be withstood
yet learned he could survive; he watched his heart
as father watches son, mature.

He grew familiar with nameless deprivations,
sunless and obscure as endless night.
He sent his soul obediently away
since it had come of age, so that it might

now dwell beside its bridegroom and its king;
and now bereft of all he stayed behind
where loneliness exceeded everything,
yet never craved the words of humankind.

And as the years grew on, and through all this,
when tenderness was needed he had learned
the joy of knowing that he held it in his hands;
entrusting all to them, as did the creatures.

DIE BETTLER

Du wußtest nicht, was den Haufen
ausmacht. Ein Fremder fand
Bettler darin. Sie verkaufen
das Hohle aus ihrer Hand.

Sie zeigen dem Hergereisten
ihren Mund voll Mist,
und er darf (er kann es sich leisten)
sehn, wie ihr Aussatz frißt.

Es zergeht in ihren zerrührten
Augen sein fremdes Gesicht;
und sie freuen sich des Verführten
und speien, wenn er spricht.

FREMDE FAMILIE

So wie der Staub, der irgendwie beginnt
und nirgends ist, zu unerklärtem Zwecke
an einem leeren Morgen in der Ecke
in die man sieht, ganz rasch zu Grau gerinnt,

so bildeten sie sich, wer weiß aus was,
im letzten Augenblick vor deinen Schritten
und waren etwas Ungewisses mitten
im nassen Niederschlag der Gasse, das

nach dir verlangte. Oder nicht nach dir.
Denn eine Stimme, wie vom vorigen Jahr,
sang dich zwar an und blieb doch ein Geweine;
und eine Hand, die wie geliehen war,
kam zwar hervor und nahm doch nicht die deine.
Wer kommt denn noch? Wen meinen diese vier?

The Beggars

What are these – contained in this cluster?
   Beggars, the visitor sees.
Thin arms reach out and they offer
hands cupped in the shape of a plea.

Finger to mouth they will show you
the ordure on which they must feast –
this privileged stranger should know
how greedily leprosy eats.

His foreignness melts, decomposes
just as their eyes decompose.
They see he is lost and this pleases:
they spit at his speech, at his clothes.

Family of Strangers

Just like the dust which seems to come from nowhere –
   nowhere until all at once
   a shadow-film of grey appears
dimming the sunlit corner where you glance –

they too appeared from god-knows-where; then
there they were before your very feet:
mysteriously-present creatures that
waited in the roadway, in the rain

and seemed to seek you – or they sought someone.
The hand which reached out did not quite belong
and though it touched you did not take your own;
then you could hear a voice begin to sing –
a voice like last year's voice. It seemed to weep.
What can they mean, these four? Whom do they seek?

LEICHEN-WÄSCHE

Sie hatten sich an ihn gewöhnt. Doch als
die Küchenlampe kam und unruhig brannte
im dunkeln Luftzug, war der Unbekannte
ganz unbekannt. Sie wuschen seinen Hals,

und da sie nichts von seinem Schicksal wußten,
so logen sie ein anderes zusamm,
fortwährend waschend. Eine mußte husten
und ließ solang den schweren Essigschwamm

auf dem Gesicht. Da gab es eine Pause
auch für die zweite. Aus der harten Bürste
klopften die Tropfen; während seine grause
gekrampfte Hand dem ganzen Hause
beweisen wollte, daß ihn nicht mehr dürste.

Und er bewies. Sie nahmen wie betreten
eiliger jetzt mit einem kurzen Huster
die Arbeit auf, so daß an den Tapeten
ihr krummer Schatten in dem stummen Muster

sich wand und wälzte wie in einem Netze,
bis daß die Waschenden zu Ende kamen.
Die Nacht im vorhanglosen Fensterrahmen
war rücksichtslos. Und einer ohne Namen
lag bar und reinlich da und gab Gesetze.

EINE VON DEN ALTEN
PARIS

Abends manchmal (weißt du, wie das tut?)
wenn sie plötzlich stehn und rückwärts nicken
und ein Lächeln, wie aus lauter Flicken,
zeigen unter ihrem halben Hut.

192

Washing the Corpse

They had grown used to him until they fetched
the kitchen lamp and set its flame, unsteady,
in the draughty darkness – for the stranger
seemed immediately to change again

into a total stranger. They washed his neck
and knowing nothing of his history
they cobbled up a story made of lies
and paused to gossip as they scrubbed at him.

One of them paused to cough. She laid the sponge,
heavy with vinegar, upon his face. The other
waited. Water pattered from her scrubbing-
brush, although his cramped and ghastly hand
wanted the world to know his thirst was gone.

They saw and understood. They coughed uneasily.
Hastily they took up the task again
so that the crooked shadows thrashed about
held in the silence of the papered walls

as if caught up within a net of pattern;
and then eventually their work was done.
Within the window-frame the night
seemed unconcerned. Meanwhile the nameless one
lay scoured and naked, judging everything.

One of the Old Women
Paris

Sometimes at evening, suddenly they start
up – beckoning you on to follow;
you can make out a tattered patched-up smile
half-hidden underneath the half-a-hat.

Neben ihnen ist dann ein Gebäude,
endlos, und sie locken dich entlang
mit dem Rätsel ihrer Räude,
mit dem Hut, dem Umhang und dem Gang.

Mit der Hand, die hinten unterm Kragen
heimlich wartet und verlangt nach dir:
wie um deine Hände einzuschlagen
in ein aufgehobenes Papier.

DER BLINDE
PARIS

Sieh, er geht und unterbricht die Stadt,
die nicht ist auf seiner dunkeln Stelle,
wie ein dunkler Sprung durch eine helle
Tasse geht. Und wie auf einem Blatt

ist auf ihm der Widerschein der Dinge
aufgemalt; er nimmt ihn nicht hinein.
Nur sein Fühlen rührt sich, so als finge
es die Welt in kleinen Wellen ein:

eine Stille, einen Widerstand –,
und dann scheint er wartend wen zu wählen:
hingegeben hebt er seine Hand,
festlich fast, wie um sich zu vermählen.

EINE WELKE

Leicht, wie nach ihrem Tode
trägt sie die Handschuh, das Tuch.
Ein Duft aus ihrer Kommode
verdrängte den lieben Geruch,

There is the wall that goes on endlessly
and always there will be the force that draws
you on, burning to solve the mystery:
who are they in their cloaks, their hats, their sores?

Why does her hand stay hidden in her collar,
why does she seem to want to entice you near –
is it to make a parcel of your hands,
to wrap them in the paper she has scavenged?

The Blind Man
Paris

Watch how he goes, proceeding through the city
(which does not reach his darkness, there within),
leaving a dark trace like a crack in porcelain.
Reflected on his surfaces you see

an image of all things, reversed, in negative,
which touches him no deeper than his skin.
And yet sensation stirs in him, as if
the World sent little waves which he takes in:

a stillness, a resistance of some kind.
Whom shall he choose? He pauses to decide
then makes a courtly gesture with his hand –
as one might wave in greeting to his bride.

A Faded Lady

As if already dead
she carries gloves and scarf.
A cupboard-smell has veiled
the dear, familiar breath

an dem sie sich früher erkannte.
Jetzt fragte sie lange nicht, wer
sie sei (: eine ferne Verwandte),
und geht in Gedanken umher

und sorgt für ein ängstliches Zimmer,
das sie ordnet und schont,
weil es vielleicht noch immer
dasselbe Mädchen bewohnt.

ABENDMAHL

Ewiges will zu uns. Wer hat die Wahl
und trennt die großen und geringen Kräfte?
Erkennst du durch das Dämmern der Geschäfte
im klaren Hinterraum das Abendmahl:

wie sie sichs halten und wie sie sichs reichen
und in der Handlung schlicht und schwer beruhn.
Aus ihren Händen heben sich die Zeichen;
sie wissen nicht, daß sie sie tun

und immer neu mit irgendwelchen Worten
einsetzen, was man trinkt und was man teilt.
Denn da ist keiner, der nicht allerorten
heimlich von hinnen geht, indem er weilt.

Und sitzt nicht immer einer unter ihnen,
der seine Eltern, die ihm ängstlich dienen,
wegschenkt an ihre abgetane Zeit?
(Sie zu verkaufen, ist ihm schon zu weit.)

which once could reassure her
of her identity –
some relative or other?
She moves in memories,

keeps her room neat and cared-for
and dusts away the fears –
in case the girl she was
still lives – and still lives there.

At Supper

E ternal patterns haunt us: who can tell
 the trivial forces from the ones that count?
Can you make out behind the darkened shop-front
the bright back-parlour where they eat their meal?

See how they sit, watch how they pass the plates
with gestures economical and grave:
the hands send messages, communicate
yet have no knowledge of the signs they give

and meanwhile they converse; continually
words interrupt the provender they share
(each one of them in spirit miles away
while on the face of it so present there).

Is there not always one who sits and stares
sullenly, though his parents try to please?
To sell them off might be to go too far:
he posts them back along their dusty years.

DIE BRANDSTÄTTE

Gemieden von dem Frühherbstmorgen, der
mißtrauisch war, lag hinter den versengten
Hauslinden, die das Heidehaus beengten,
ein Neues, Leeres. Eine Stelle mehr,

auf welcher Kinder, von Gott weiß woher,
einander zuschrien und nach Fetzen haschten.
Doch alle wurden stille, sooft er,
der Sohn von hier, aus heißen, halbveraschten

Gebälken Kessel und verbogne Tröge
an einem langen Gabelaste zog, –
um dann mit einem Blick als ob er löge
die andern anzusehn, die er bewog

zu glauben, was an dieser Stelle stand.
Denn seit es nicht mehr war, schien es ihm so
seltsam: phantastischer als Pharao.
Und er war anders. Wie aus fernem Land.

DIE GRUPPE
PARIS

Als pflückte einer rasch zu einem Strauß:
ordnet der Zufall hastig die Gesichter,
lockert sie auf und drückt sie wieder dichter,
ergreift zwei ferne, läßt ein nahes aus,

tauscht das mit dem, bläst irgendeines frisch,
wirft einen Hund, wie Kraut, aus dem Gemisch
und zieht, was niedrig schaut, wie durch verworrne
Stiele und Blätter, an dem Kopf nach vorne

und bindet es ganz klein am Rande ein;
und streckt sich wieder, ändert und verstellt
und hat nur eben Zeit, zum Augenschein

After the Fire

The autumn sunshine seemed suspicious of
   whatever lay behind those leaf-scorched limes.
Where once had stood the cottage on the moors,
nothing but emptiness: a space. Above

its ashes, children sprung from god-knows-where
cried out like jackdaws as they rummaged for
whatever they might find. Each time the lad
whose home it was, hunting among the charred

half-buried timbers, fished with his long forked pole,
drew out ruined pots, half-melted kettles,
a silence fell. Then he would turn his face
and as if guiltily look at the others:

he must make them believe what had stood here –
for now that it was gone it seemed so strange,
as fabulous as some dynastic king.
And he himself was changed. A creature from afar.

The Group
Paris

Like someone in a hurry gathering flowers,
   chance picks the faces and arranges them –
lets some hang down, packs others tight and trim,
chooses what's distant yet rejects what's near,

switches them round and puffs the dust from some,
expels a dog – a weed – from the ensemble,
brings up to light what's hidden or obscured
grasping their heads to draw them gently forward

through crowded leaves, and lightly binds the stems;
then reaches out adjusting this and that
till there remains just barely enough time

zurückzuspringen mitten auf die Matte,
auf der im nächsten Augenblick der glatte
Gewichteschwinger seine Schwere schwellt.

SCHLANGEN-BESCHWÖRUNG

Wenn auf dem Markt, sich wiegend, der Beschwörer
die Kürbisflöte pfeift, die reizt und lullt,
so kann es sein, daß er sich einen Hörer
herüberlockt, der ganz aus dem Tumult

der Buden eintritt in den Kreis der Pfeife,
die will und will und will und die erreicht,
daß das Reptil in seinem Korb sich steife
und die das steife schmeichlerisch erweicht,

abwechselnd immer schwindelnder und blinder
mit dem was schreckt und streckt, und dem, was löst –;
und dann genügt ein Blick: so hat der Inder
dir eine Fremde eingeflößt,

in der du stirbst. Es ist als überstürze
glühender Himmel dich. Es geht ein Sprung
durch dein Gesicht. Es legen sich Gewürze
auf deine nordische Erinnerung,

die dir nichts hilft. Dich feien keine Kräfte,
die Sonne gärt, das Fieber fällt und trifft;
von böser Freude steilen sich die Schäfte,
und in den Schlangen glänzt das Gift.

to take one quick step back, for one last glance –
to step onto the mat on which at once
the strapping Strong Man stands and wields his weights.

Snake-Charmer

Rocking upon his heels the sorcerer plays
upon his calabash, and whines and soothes
drawing, perhaps, a stranger from the noisy
market-crowd among the stalls and booths

into the sorcerer's-circle of his flute
whose note insists, insists, insists, but when
the snake stands upright, rigid, in its basket
must melt it into fluency again,

harsh notes, to stretch and stiffen, giving way
while all grows wilder, blinder, dizzier,
to softer music that can liquefy…
With one look you are hypnotised and near

to drowning in this strangeness…now you feel
descend upon your head the burning sky.
Your face cracks like a jug. Hot spices kill
the taste of every northern memory

and nothing now protects you, can defend.
Hot sun ferments, a fever strikes you down,
the shafts of manic evil still ascend
and in the serpents all the poisons shine.

SCHWARZE KATZE

Ein Gespenst ist noch wie eine Stelle,
dran dein Blick mit einem Klange stößt;
aber da, an diesem schwarzen Felle
wird dein stärkstes Schauen aufgelöst:

wie ein Tobender, wenn er in vollster
Raserei ins Schwarze stampft,
jählings am benehmenden Gepolster
einer Zelle aufhört und verdampft.

Alle Blicke, die sie jemals trafen,
scheint sie also an sich zu verhehlen,
um darüber drohend und verdrossen
zuzuschauern und damit zu schlafen.
Doch auf einmal kehrt sie, wie geweckt,
ihr Gesicht und mitten in das deine:
und da triffst du deinen Blick im geelen
Amber ihrer runden Augensteine
unerwartet wieder: eingeschlossen
wie ein ausgestorbenes Insekt.

VOR-OSTERN
NEAPEL

Morgen wird in diesen tiefgekerbten
Gassen, die sich durch getürmtes Wohnen
unten dunkel nach dem Hafen drängen,
hell das Gold der Prozessionen rollen;
statt der Fetzen werden die ererbten
Bettbezüge, welche wehen wollen,
von den immer höheren Balkonen
(wie in Fließendem gespiegelt) hängen.

Black Cat

A ghost is still a presence in a place;
  your sight can strike it and can make it sound.
But when they fall upon this coal-black pelt
even the fiercest looks are melted down:

as when one stamps and rages, in some hell
of lunatic black rage,
the madness may evaporate, be stilled
within the nowhere of a padded cage.

It is as if she took and hid away
all of the looks that ever fell on her
and hoards them jealously, suspiciously,
and like a miser counts them night and day.
But all at once, alerted, she will face
around and meet you eye to eye:
caught in that golden stare you suddenly
are given back, imprisoned, motionless,
yourself reflected there, in amber
like some long-extinct insect.

Easter Market
Naples

Tomorrow, in the deeply-sunken alleys
  pushing past the crowded tenements
you will see the shining golden pageant
moving towards the harbour; for its banners
ancient bedlinen already flutters
like reflections upon moving water,
hanging down from all the balconies
steeply rising, piled upon each other.

Aber heute hämmert an den Klopfern
jeden Augenblick ein voll Bepackter,
und sie schleppen immer neue Käufe;
dennoch stehen strotzend noch die Stände.
An der Ecke zeigt ein aufgehackter
Ochse seine frischen Innenwände,
und in Fähnchen enden allen Läufe.
Und ein Vorrat wie von tausend Opfern

drängt auf Bänken, hängt sich rings um Pflöcke,
zwängt sich, wölbt sich, wälzt sich aus dem Dämmer
aller Türen, und vor dem Gegähne
der Melonen strecken sich die Brote.
Voller Gier und Handlung ist das Tote;
doch viel stiller sind die jungen Hähne
und die abgehängten Ziegenböcke
und am allerleisesten die Lämmer,

die die Knaben um die Schultern nehmen
und die willig von den Schritten nicken;
während in der Mauer der verglasten
spanischen Madonna die Agraffe
und das Silber in den Diademen
von dem Lichter-Vorgefühl beglänzter
schimmert. Aber drüber in dem Fenster
ziegt sich blickverschwenderisch ein Affe
und führt rasch in einer angemaßten
Haltung Gesten aus, die sich nicht schicken.

DER BALKON
NEAPEL

Von der Enge, oben, des Balkones
angeordnet wie von einem Maler
und gebunden wie zu einem Strauß
alternder Gesichter und ovaler,
klar im Abend, sehn sie idealer,
rührender und wie für immer aus.

But today, heavy-laden hawkers
hammer at door-knockers, ordinary people
stagger homewards with their purchases,
and the stalls stay crammed with produce still.
At a corner-stall a butchered steer
shows the world his scoured-out emptiness,
legs which starkly end in frills of paper.
As if for a thousand sacrifices

offerings hang on racks, are heaped on trestles,
spilling out from every dim-lit entrance:
boxes, barrels, bulging sacks and baskets,
loaves of bread stretch out in rigid rows
while behind them lie the yawning melons.
All these lifeless things seem frantic, anxious
to engage in commerce. Much more quiet
are the hanging goats and cockerels

and especially the lambs
dangling from boys' shoulders, nodding heads,
at each step assenting to their fate.
In the wall behind the glazed partition
of the Spanish statue of the Virgin,
silver clasps and silver diadems
shine, anticipating Easter light.
But a monkey in a window leans
out and strikes various attitudes
and makes rapid gestures, all obscene.

The Balcony
Naples

The narrow balcony decides their places
as if a painter had arranged them there
choosing and binding them in his bouquet
of ageing and of young, more oval, faces
idealised by a clear evening light
making them poignant, as if there for ever:

Diese aneinander angelehnten
Schwestern, die, als ob sie sich von weit
ohne Aussicht nacheinander sehnten,
lehnen, Einsamkeit an Einsamkeit;

und der Bruder mit dem feierlichen
Schweigen, zugeschlossen, voll Geschick,
doch von einem sanften Augenblick
mit der Mutter unbemerkt verglichen;

und dazwischen, abgelebt und länglich,
längst mit keinem mehr verwandt,
einer Greisin Maske, unzugänglich,
wie im Fallen von der einen Hand

aufgehalten, während eine zweite
welkere, als ob sie weitergleite,
unten vor den Kleidern hängt zur Seite

von dem Kinder-Angesicht,
das das Letzte ist, versucht, verblichen,
von den Stäben wieder durchgestrichen
wie noch unbestimmbar, wie noch nicht.

AUSWANDERER-SCHIFF
NEAPEL

Denk: daß einer heiß und glühend flüchte,
und die Sieger wären hinterher,
und auf einmal machte der
Flüchtende kurz, unerwartet, Kehr
gegen Hunderte –: so sehr
warf sich das Erglühende der Früchte
immer wieder an das blaue Meer:

206

leant against one another stand the sisters
as if, still separate and far-removed,
they pined, bereft of hope, for one another
supporting solitude on solitude,

while in tongue-tied dignity their brother,
locked within himself, a man of destiny,
momentarily looks like their mother,
a gentler look which passes by unseen;

between them, life-worn and attenuated,
no longer kin to anybody living,
the mask of an old woman, alienated,
one clutching hand alone saves her from falling,

another even more withered-looking hand
hangs down against her dress like something foreign,
arrested there from sliding to the ground

beside the last: the child whose face and figure,
bleached pale, are tentative and so unsure
that iron railings strike them out again
as unsubstantiated – not yet there.

Emigrant Ship
Naples

Picture a scene: one flees while his pursuers
follow behind and gain remorselessly
until he halts – and unexpectedly
facing about confronts them fiercely
though all alone, outnumbered by their scores...
With just such bravery the glowing colours
of the fruit contend against blue sea

als das langsame Orangen-Boot
sie vorübertrug bis an das große
graue Schiff, zu dem, von Stoß zu Stoße,
andre Boote Fische hoben, Brot, –
während es, voll Hohn, in seinem Schooße
Kohlen aufnahm, offen wie der Tod.

LANDSCHAFT

Wie zuletzt, in einem Augenblick
aufgehäuft aus Hängen, Häusern, Stücken
alter Himmel und zerbrochnen Brücken,
und von drüben her, wie vom Geschick,
von dem Sonnenuntergang getroffen,
angeschuldigt, aufgerissen, offen –
ginge dort die Ortschaft tragisch aus:

fiele nicht auf einmal in das Wunde,
drin zerfließend, aus der nächsten Stunde
jener Tropfen kühlen Blaus,
der die Nacht schon in den Abend mischt,
so daß das von ferne Angefachte
sachte, wie erlöst, erlischt.

Ruhig sind die Tore und die Bogen,
durchsichtige Wolken wogen
über blassen Häuserreihn
die schon Dunkel in sich eingesogen;
aber plötzlich ist vom Mond ein Schein
durchgeglitten, licht, als hätte ein
Erzengel irgendwo sein Schwert gezogen.

as the orange-boat laboriously ferries
passengers across, at last to berth
at th.: grey ship, boats bobbing beneath it
unregarded, loading loaves and fishes
while its belly fills with coals, exposes
all; as undisguised and stark as death.

Townscape

All at once, piles of heaped-up buildings
and escarpments and the broken fragments
of the ancient skies, the shattered bridges,
unprotected and exposed, lie threatened
by the orange flames of sunset –
the whole city sentenced to destruction
as if fate had destined it for this:

then a touch of blue, like healing lotion
twilight mixed with darkness might provide,
bathes the wound and, later, softly quenching,
cools the angry fire which the sun
has already kindled; leaves the town
quiet and at peace, as if reprieved.

Empty colonnades and silent gateways.
Vast translucent cloudbanks billow
over streets whose pallid houses
wait in rows and drink the darkness.
Suddenly a shaft of moonlight
shines out fiercely, as if somewhere
the archangel had unsheathed his brilliant sword.

RÖMISCHE CAMPAGNA

Aus der vollgestellten Stadt, die lieber
schliefe, träumend von den hohen Thermen,
geht der grade Gräberweg ins Fieber;
und die Fenster in den letzten Fermen

sehn ihm nach mit einem bösen Blick.
Und er hat sie immer im Genick,
wenn er hingeht, rechts und links zerstörend,
bis er draußen atemlos beschwörend

seine Leere zu den Himmeln hebt,
hastig um sich schauend, ob ihn keine
Fenster treffen. Während er den weiten

Aquädukten zuwinkt herzuschreiten,
geben ihm die Himmel für die seine
ihre Leere, die ihn überlebt.

LIED VOM MEER
CAPRI. PICCOLA MARINA

Uraltes Wehn vom Meer,
Meerwind bei Nacht:
du kommst zu keinem her;
wenn einer wacht,
so muß er sehn, wie er
dich übersteht:
uraltes Wehn vom Meer,
welches weht
nur wie für Ur-Gestein,
lauter Raum
reißend von weit herein...
O wie fühlt dich ein
treibender Feigenbaum
oben im Mondschein.

Roman Campagna

Leaving the packed city which would rather
dream of ardent springs high in the mountains,
the high-road to the graveyard, steep as fever,
fleeing the malice aimed towards it hastens

onwards, leaving the last windows glaring
after and their violence, unrelenting,
blasting all that lies on either side;
breathless now, finally entreats the wide

heavens – raising up its empty hands:
Nothing! Now it glances round
to see if windows watch it. While it beckons

the aqueducts approaching in the distance,
heaven rewards it with an emptiness
which will outlast it, which will never end.

Song of the Sea
Capri, Piccola Marina

Primeval breath, sea-wind
that blows at night
obeying no command;
those who watch late
must learn how to withstand
your subtle power:
sea-breath, primeval wind
blowing here
as if to inspire old stones
forcing in
sheer space, gathered afar.

What does the fig-tree learn
whose branches your breath stirs
up there, beneath the moon?

NÄCHTLICHE FAHRT
SANKT PETERSBURG

Damals als wir mit den glatten Trabern
(schwarzen, aus dem Orloff'schen Gestüt) –,
während hinter hohen Kandelabern
Stadtnachtfronten lagen, angefrüht,
stumm und keiner Stunde mehr gemäß –,
fuhren, nein: vergingen oder flogen
und um lastende Paläste bogen
in das Wehn der Newa-Quais,

hingerissen durch das wache Nachten,
das nicht Himmel und nicht Erde hat, –
als das Drängende von unbewachten
Gärten gärend aus dem Ljetnij-Ssad
aufstieg, während seine Steinfiguren
schwindend mit ohnmächtigen Konturen
hinter uns vergingen, wie wir fuhren –:

damals hörte diese Stadt
auf zu sein. Auf einmal gab sie zu,
daß sie niemals war, um nichts als Ruh
flehend; wie ein Irrer, dem das Wirrn
plötzlich sich entwirrt, das ihn verriet,
und der einen jahrelangen kranken
gar nicht zu verwandelnden Gedanken,
den er nie mehr denken muß: Granit –
aus dem leeren schwankenden Gehirn
fallen fühlt, bis man ihn nicht mehr sieht.

PAPAGEIEN-PARK
JARDIN DES PLANTES, PARIS

Unter türkischen Linden, die blühen, an Rasenrändern,
in leise von ihrem Heimweh geschaukelten Ständern
atmen die Ara und wissen von ihren Ländern,
die sich, auch wenn sie nicht hinsehn, nicht verändern.

Night Drive
St Petersburg

That was when, behind the trotting horses
(glossy blacks bred from the Orloff stud)
there were tall street-gas-lamps and the houses
lying dark (brushed by faintest light but
lifeless, answering to none),
and as we drove, but no! as we were flown
in a curve around the massive palaces
to the river Neva's windswept quays,

past the rank and brooding Summer Gardens
lying abandoned, restless, overgrown;
while the night observed us racing on
through the darkness over earth and sky, we
glimpsed the drunken statues reeling past,
let them fade behind us till at last
melting into blackness they were gone...

But the city suddenly surrenders
now pretending that it never was,
craving nothing more, at last, than peace:
as a madman feeling madness cease
suddenly recovering sanity
finds himself again, feels some obsession
borne for years and heavy as a stone
loosen, of a sudden fall away,
leave him swiftly cured and quite at ease:
healed, delivered, mind and spirit freed.

The Parrot House
Jardin des Plantes, Paris

Under the flowering limes at the edge of the lawns,
balanced on perches that silently rock with their yearning
they breathe in the alien air, always remembering
their homeland; distant, unseen and forever unchanging.

Fremd im beschäftigten Grünen wie eine Parade,
zieren sie sich und fühlen sich selber zu schade,
und mit den kostbaren Schnäbeln aus Jaspis und Jade
kauen sie Graues, verschleudern es, finden es fade.

Unten klauben die duffen Tauben, was sie nicht mögen,
während sich oben die höhnischen Vögel verbeugen
zwischen den beiden fast leeren vergeudeten Trögen.

Aber dann wiegen sie wieder und schläfern und äugen,
spielen mit dunkelen Zungen, die gerne lögen,
zerstreut an den Fußfesselringen. Warten auf Zeugen.

DIE PARKE

I

Unaufhaltsam heben sich die Parke
 aus dem sanft zerfallenden Vergehn;
überhäuft mit Himmeln, überstarke
Überlieferte, die überstehn,

um sich auf den klaren Rasenplänen
auszubreiten und zurückzuziehn,
immer mit demselben souveränen
Aufwand, wie beschützt durch ihn,

und den unerschöpflichen Erlös
königlicher Größe noch vermehrend,
aus sich steigend, in sich wiederkehrend:
huldvoll, prunkend, purpurn und pompös.

Too precious for everyday life in the trees, as exotic,
as foreign, as actors, they preen and attend to their costumes;
exquisite beaks fashioned of jade and of jasper
chew on the tasteless grey stuff they deliberately squander.

Below them, pedestrian pigeons peck up what lies scattered,
while they scornfully stoop between troughs
with little or nothing left in them, the contents rejected.

They go back to their brooding; rocking and leering; letting
livid tongues, dark and mendacious, absently
play with the chains of their shackles: wait for their audience.

The Royal Parks

I

Enduring history, its soft decay,
tall and impregnable the parks survive:
with too much wealth, above them too much sky,
with too much stamina, too long a life,

alternately they swell themselves and grow
to lucent lawns and then again withdraw
preserving the unchanging luxury
which still safeguards, protects unchangingly;

through usury continually increasing
the splendour and rewards of mighty kings
they rise above themselves, return again
in royal purple, proud, magnificent.

II

Leise von den Alleen
ergriffen, rechts und links,
folgend dem Weitergehen
irgend eines Winks,

trittst du mit einem Male
in das Beisammensein
einer schattigen Wasserschale
mit vier Bänken aus Stein;

in eine abgetrennte
Zeit, die allein vergeht.
Auf feuchte Postamente,
auf denen nichts mehr steht,

hebst du einen tiefen
erwartenden Atemzug;
während das silberne Triefen
von dem dunkeln Bug

dich schon zu den Seinen
zählt und weiterspricht.
Und du fühlst dich unter Steinen
die hören, und rührst dich nicht.

III

Den Teichen und den eingerahmten Weihern
verheimlicht man noch immer das Verhör
der Könige. Sie warten unter Schleiern,
und jeden Augenblick kann Monseigneur

vorüberkommen; und dann wollen sie
des Königs Laune oder Trauer mildern
und von den Marmorrändern wieder die
Teppiche mit alten Spiegelbildern

II

S oftly held by pathways,
    hedges left and right,
following, your eyes
fixed upon some sight

you find yourself encroaching
suddenly upon
a dripping, shaded basin
flanked by seats of stone:

there the passing hours
spend themselves alone
and you stare at columns
whose statues have long gone;

apprehensive, watchful,
you await what may befall
knowing the silver trickle
falling from the bowl

counts you as its own now,
murmuring on and on
while the stones around you
listen: you are stone.

III

T he silvered lakes, the calm protected ponds,
    hear nothing of the sentencing of kings.
They keep their veils and wait, for presently
great Monseigneur might call

and then their pleasure and their task must be
to raise royal spirits or to lighten grief;
then from their marble banks they must unroll
again the ancient tapestries

hinunterhängen, wie um einen Platz:
auf grünem Grund, mit Silber, Rosa, Grau,
gewährtem Weiß und leicht gerührtem Blau
und einem Könige und einer Frau
und Blumen in dem wellenden Besatz.

IV

Und Natur, erlaucht und als verletze
sie nur unentschloßnes Ungefähr,
nahm von diesen Königen Gesetze,
selber selig, um den Tapis-vert

ihrer Bäume Traum und Übertreibung
aufzutürmen aus gebauschtem Grün
und die Abende nach der Beschreibung
von Verliebten in die Avenün

einzumalen mit dem weichen Pinsel,
der ein firnisklares aufgelöstes
Lächeln glänzend zu enthalten schien:

der Natur ein liebes, nicht ihr größtes,
aber eines, das sie selbst verliehn,
um auf rosenvoller Liebes-Insel
es zu einem größern aufzuziehn.

V

Götter von Alleen und Altanen,
niemals ganzgeglaubte Götter, die
altern in den gradbeschnittnen Bahnen,
höchstens angelächelte Dianen
wenn die königliche Venerie

to hang them out as if reflected in
the panes of windows in a city square:
a ground of green, with silver, rose and grey
and with a little white, a touch of blue,
and with a king, and with a lady too,
and scalloped, flower-patterned bordering.

IV

Nature, exalted, seems the enemy
only of what is unresolved or mean;
looking to kings for her instructions
she joyfully erects upon green lawns

the bushy altitudes of dreaming trees
and in her fondness, generously
takes up her softest brush and swiftly draws
the kind of sunset only lovers see,

proudly displays it in the avenues
under a brilliant glaze which seems to glow
as if her varnishes contained a smile...

one dear to Nature, not her greatest joy
but one that she herself was given
for her to nurture on some rose-crammed isle
and watch it grow into maturity.

V

Gods of the leafy avenues and terraces,
hoarding their years and lichens in green aisles,
no longer prayed to, scarcely held divine;
Dianas who were looked upon with smiles
when like a storm some royal venery,
urgent and over-loud, peremptory,

wie ein Wind die hohen Morgen teilend
aufbrach, übereilt und übereilend –;
höchstens angelächelte, doch nie
angeflehte Götter. Elegante
Pseudonyme, unter denen man
sich verbarg und blühte oder brannte, –
leichtgeneigte, lächelnd angewandte
Götter, die noch manchmal dann und wann

das gewähren, was sie einst gewährten,
wenn das Blühen der entzückten Gärten
ihnen ihre kalte Haltung nimmt;
wenn sie ganz von ersten Schatten beben
und Versprechen um Versprechen geben,
alle unbegrenzt und unbestimmt.

VI

Fühlst du, wie keiner von allen
    Wegen steht und stockt;
von gelassenen Treppen fallen,
durch ein Nichts von Neigung
leise weitergelockt,
über alle Terrassen
die Wege, zwischen den Massen
verlangsamt und gelenkt,
bis zu den weiten Teichen,
wo sie (wie einem Gleichen)
der reiche Park verschenkt
an den reichen Raum: den Einen,
der mit Scheinen und Widerscheinen
seinen Besitz durchdringt,
aus dem er von allen Seiten
Weiten mit sich bringt,
wenn er aus schließenden Weihern
zu wolkigen Abendfeiern
sich in die Himmel schwingt.

fractured the silence of the awaking days...
masked as such gods mankind might bloom or blaze;
unworshipped gods, become curiosities
or pseudonyms or fashionable disguise
even though they from time to time extend

the services they long ago conferred:
sometimes the blossoming, enchanted gardens
will kindle them anew, and sometimes they,
under the early light, the dawning shade,
tremble to life and promise lavishly
numberless miracles unspecified.

VI

Notice how the pathways
wander, never cease
casually descending
without urgency
terraces and stairways,
passing banks of flowers,
pausing for direction
they continue on
till they reach the margins
where the lakes extend;
there the prosperous parkland
makes a gift of them
as if to an equal
to the emptiness
gleaming and reflecting
through the great estate,
conjuring on all sides
further distances;
as the water darkens
and the evening starts
celebrating, feasting,
vaulting to the skies.

Aber Schalen sind, drin der Najaden
Spiegelbilder, die sie nicht mehr baden,
wie ertrunken liegen, sehr verzerrt;
die Alleen sind durch Balustraden
in der Ferne wie versperrt.

Immer geht ein feuchter Blätterfall
durch die Luft hinunter wie auf Stufen,
jeder Vogelruf ist wie verrufen,
wie vergiftet jede Nachtigall.

Selbst der Frühling ist da nicht mehr gebend,
diese Büsche glauben nicht an ihn;
ungern duftet trübe, überlebend
abgestandener Jasmin

alt und mit Zerfallendem vermischt.
Mit dir weiter rückt ein Bündel Mücken,
so als würde hinter deinem Rücken
alles gleich vernichtet und verwischt.

BILDNIS

Daß von dem verzichtenden Gesichte
keiner ihrer großen Schmerzen fiele,
trägt sie langsam durch die Trauerspiele
ihrer Züge schönen welken Strauß,
wild gebunden und schon beinah lose;
manchmal fällt, wie eine Tuberose,
ein verlornes Lächeln müd heraus.

Und sie geht gelassen drüber hin,
müde, mit den schönen blinden Händen,
welche wissen, daß sie es nicht fänden, –

B ut there are basins which still hold reflections
though water-nymphs no longer come to bathe;
their images lie drowned and twisted, broken,
and now the distant avenues are glimpsed
as if imprisoned, held by balustrades.

And all the time the damp dead leaves descend
and step by step they flutter to the ground.
As if maliciously the birds still call;
corruption sings within the nightingale.

Here even springtime could not lend its blessing
to tired growth, demoralised and grey;
a stubborn scent survives of jasmine
no longer fresh, part sweetness, part decay.

Now as you stroll a cloud of insects gathers
and stays with you as you continue on.
You know for certain that when you have passed
all this will be extinguished; all be gone.

Portrait

U nwilling that the look of self-denial
should tell the whole world of her private sorrows,
she holds the faded posy of her features
(artlessly bound and now fatigued and pale)
attentively through the long tragedies –
but sometimes like a single tuberose
a smile is lost from it, escapes and falls:

she passes negligently over it,
weary and, with her lovely sightless hands
knowing they never can recover it, resigned

223

und sie sagt Erdichtetes, darin
Schicksal schwankt, gewolltes, irgendeines,
und sie giebt ihm ihrer Seele Sinn,
daß es ausbricht wie ein Ungemeines:
wie das Schreien eines Steines –

und sie läßt, mit hochgehobnem Kinn,
alle diese Worte wieder fallen,
ohne bleibend; denn nicht eins von allen
ist der wehen Wirklichkeit gemäß,
ihrem einzigen Eigentum,
das sie, wie ein fußloses Gefäß,
halten muß, hoch über ihren Ruhm
und den Gang der Abende hinaus.

VENEZIANISCHER MORGEN
RICHARD BEER-HOFMANN ZUGEEIGNET

Fürstlich verwöhnte Fenster sehen immer,
    was manchesmal uns zu bemühn geruht:
die Stadt, die immer wieder, wo ein Schimmer
von Himmel trifft auf ein Gefühl von Flut,

sich bildet ohne irgendwann zu sein.
Ein jeder Morgen muß ihr die Opale
erst zeigen, die sie gestern trug, und Reihn
von Spiegelbildern ziehn aus dem Kanale
und sie erinnern an die andern Male:
dann giebt sie sich erst zu und fällt sich ein

wie eine Nymphe, die den Zeus empfing.
Das Ohrgehäng erklingt an ihrem Ohre;
sie aber hebt San Giorgio Maggiore
und lächelt lässig in das schöne Ding.

she speaks her lines (the fickleness of fate,
contrived and commonplace) enriching all,
expressing the uniqueness of her heart
offering her own extraordinary soul:
the grief, the lamentation of a stone!

She lets the words fall from her upraised face
content to let them pass; for none of them
can measure up to raw reality
which stays her only true possession
and which, like a vase without a base,
she is obliged to carry constantly
with her – lifting it high above her fame,
above the evenings moving in procession.

Venetian Morning

Tall windows regally command the view
which we can only sometimes look upon:
the city tentatively made anew
each time the sky lets its reflections shine

upon a gleam of tide – ever redrawn
yet never quite achieved. Each morning she
requires the heavens to show her once again
the opals which she wore the previous day,
and every morning her canals present
the images which are her memories.

She gives herself, her chiming ornaments
(an amorous nymph surrendering to the God),
lifts up San Giorgio above the flood
and smiles and gazes, lazily content.

SPÄTHERBST IN VENEDIG

Nun treibt die Stadt schon nicht mehr wie ein Köder,
der alle aufgetauchten Tage fängt.
Die gläsernen Paläste klingen spröder
an deinen Blick. Und aus den Gärten hängt

der Sommer wie ein Haufen Marionetten
kopfüber, müde, umgebracht.
Aber vom Grund aus alten Waldskeletten
steigt Willen auf: als sollte über Nacht

der General des Meeres die Galeeren
verdoppeln in dem wachen Arsenal,
um schon die nächste Morgenluft zu teeren

mit einer Flotte, welche ruderschlagend
sich drängt und jäh, mit allen Flaggen tagend,
den großen Wind hat, strahlend und fatal.

SAN MARCO
VENEDIG

In diesem Innern, das wie ausgehöhlt
sich wölbt und wendet in den goldnen Smalten,
rundkantig, glatt, mit Köstlichkeit geölt,
ward dieses Staates Dunkelheit gehalten

und heimlich aufgehäuft, als Gleichgewicht
des Lichtes, das in allen seinen Dingen
sich so vermehrte, daß sie fast vergingen –.
Und plötzlich zweifelst du: vergehn sie nicht?

und drängst zurück die harte Galerie,
die, wie ein Gang im Bergwerk, nah am Glanz
der Wölbung hängt; und du erkennst die heile

Late Autumn in Venice

The city now no longer casts its lure
  to capture the bright shoals of rising days.
A harsher light glares from glass palaces
and in gardens all the ruined summer

lies abandoned, stacked as if in heaps
of sprawling puppets, broken-necked; all murdered.
Yet purpose stirs in slime and rises up
as blackened spars, the bones of ancient woods –

as though by night the city's Admiral
had doubled up the galleys in the Arsenal
and made each vessel ready, rigged and armed

to put to sea and scent the dawn with tar,
the great wind meeting them outside the harbour,
flags flying, oars beating, glittering and lethal.

San Marco
Venice

Within this space, this cavern hollowed out
  with arches reaching to a golden sky
and every roughness smoothed to luxury,
was kept in store the darkness of the State

which silently increased as if required
to cancel out the brightness of the light
of all the glittering things which grow more bright
till the whole treasure seems destroyed by fire –

so that you think: How can all this endure?
Pressing along the narrow gallery
hung like a catwalk from the canopy

227

Helle des Ausblicks: aber irgendwie
wehmütig messend ihre müde Weile
am nahen Überstehn des Viergespanns.

EIN DOGE

Fremde Gesandte sahen, wie sie geizten
mit ihm und allem was er tat;
während sie ihn zu seiner Größe reizten,
umstellten sie das goldene Dogat

mit Spähern und Beschränkern immer mehr,
bange, daß nicht die Macht sie überfällt,
die sie in ihm (so wie man Löwen hält)
vorsichtig nährten. Aber er,

im Schutze seiner halbverhängten Sinne,
ward dessen nicht gewahr und hielt nicht inne,
größer zu werden. Was die Signorie

in seinem Innern zu bezwingen glaubte,
bezwang er selbst. In seinem greisen Haupte
war es besiegt. Sein Antlitz zeigte wie.

DIE LAUTE

Ich bin die Laute. Willst du meinen Leib
beschreiben, seine schön gewölbten Streifen:
sprich so, als sprächest du von einer reifen
gewölbten Feige. Übertreib

das Dunkel, das du in mir siehst. Es war
Tullias Dunkelheit. In ihrer Scham
war nicht so viel, und ihr erhelltes Haar
war wie ein heller Saal. Zuweilen nahm

you find the shining city still secure
yet somehow wearied by her history,
so nearly crushed beneath the quadriga.

The Doge

The foreign envoys saw how little space
    was granted him in any enterprise:
while they manipulated him to greatness
the golden State was set about with spies,

informers who were everywhere around him
and watched like lion-tamers that the power
vested in him, which they had nurtured there,
should not rebound upon themselves and rend them.

The Doge, with his perceptions half-obscured,
seemed to see none of this and, unrestrained,
grew all the while more great: he now controlled

all in himself that they, the Signory,
intended to control, the battle won.
His old face showed the cost of victory.

The Lute

I am the lute. If you wish to describe
  my body with its curved, voluptuous stripes,
you must seek words that will achieve a shape
as swollen as a fig, as rich, as ripe,

and you should strive to emphasise the darker
tones you see – for even Tullia's shame
was not so dark as I. Her tinted hair
shone like a sunlit room. From time to time

sie etwas Klang von meiner Oberfläche
in ihr Gesicht und sang zu mir.
Dann spannte ich mich gegen ihre Schwäche,
und endlich war mein Inneres in ihr.

DER ABENTEURER

I

Wenn er unter jene welche *waren*
trat: der Plötzliche, der *schien*,
war ein Glanz wie von Gefahren
in dem ausgesparten Raum um ihn,

den er lächelnd überschritt, um einer
Herzogin den Fächer aufzuheben:
diesen warmen Fächer, den er eben
wollte fallen sehen. Und wenn keiner

mit ihm eintrat in die Fensternische
(wo die Parke gleich ins Träumerische
stiegen, wenn er nur nach ihnen wies),
ging er lässig an die Kartentische
und gewann. Und unterließ

nicht, die Blicke alle zu behalten,
die ihn zweifelnd oder zärtlich trafen,
und auch die in Spiegel fielen, galten.
Er beschloß, auch heute nicht zu schlafen

wie die letzte lange Nacht, und bog
einen Blick mit seinem rücksichtslosen
welcher war: als hätte er von Rosen
Kinder, die man irgendwo erzog.

her face acquired its tone from me:
she sang to me like my own surfaces!
I braced myself against her frailty
and all that was in me passed into her.

The Adventurer

I

As he went about among the *real*
(he, so urgent, who could only *seem*)
like a hint of danger, like a thrill
something glittered in the spacious room

which he traversed smiling, to return
to a Duchess' hand, still warm,
the silken fan just that moment fallen,
just as he had wished. When sometimes

no-one came to stand beside him
in the window (where the insubstantial,
ghostly park drifted like a dream)
he would wander to the gaming-table
and he played and won, all the time

well aware of each watching eye
staring (doubting or admiringly)
at him, in reflection and directly.
He determined not to sleep that day,

echoing the sleepless night before,
bending looks with his own carefree gaze –
as if he had children born of roses,
growing up and flourishing somewhere.

In den Tagen – (nein, es waren keine),
da die Flut sein unterstes Verlies
ihm bestritt, als wär es nicht das seine,
und ihn, steigend, an die Steine
der daran gewöhnten Wölbung stieß,

fiel ihm plötzlich einer von den Namen
wieder ein, die er vor Zeiten trug.
Und er wußte wieder: Leben kamen,
wenn er lockte; wie im Flug

kamen sie: noch warme Leben Toter,
die er, ungeduldiger, bedrohter,
weiterlebte mitten drin;
oder die nicht ausgelebten Leben,
und er wußte sie hinaufzuheben,
und sie hatten wieder Sinn.

Oft war keine Stelle an ihm sicher,
und er zitterte: Ich bin – – –
doch im nächsten Augenblicke glich er
dem Geliebten einer Königin.

Immer wieder war ein Sein zu haben:
die Geschicke angefangner Knaben,
die, als hätte man sie nicht gewagt,
abgebrochen waren, abgesagt,
nahm er auf und riß sie in sich hin;
denn er mußte einmal nur die Gruft
solcher Aufgegebener durchschreiten,
und die Düfte ihrer Möglichkeiten
lagen wieder in der Luft.

II

In those days (but no, those were not days)
when he was embattled with the seas
contesting with them for his deepest dungeons,
he was lifted high up, to the stones
of the vaults to which their flood-tide rose,

finding that he suddenly remembered
once again a name which he once used;
and he knew that if he only beckoned
lives would come to him – as if they flew

to him from the dead but were still warm:
other, different lives, lives that someone
vulnerable and quick might make his own.
Some were lives unlived, still incomplete.
It was in his power to exalt
and to make them purposeful again.

Sometimes he owned nothing that was certain,
trembling, stammering: I fear...
then as confident a moment later
as a courtier loved by a great queen.

Always there were destinies to capture
as of boys whose lives, scarce yet begun,
had been cast away from them in terror
till he caught them up and put them on:
always, every time that he would wander
in the cemeteries of the forsaken
all the scents of what they might have been
rose to hang like pollen in the air.

FALKEN-BEIZE

Kaiser sein heißt unverwandelt vieles
überstehen bei geheimer Tat:
wenn der Kanzler nachts den Turm betrat,
fand er *ihn*, des hohen Federspieles
kühnen fürstlichen Traktat

in den eingeneigten Schreiber sagen;
denn er hatte im entlegnen Saale
selber nächtelang und viele Male
das noch ungewohnte Tier getragen,
wenn es fremd war, neu und aufgebräut.
Und er hatte dann sich nie gescheut,
Pläne, welche in ihm aufgesprungen,
oder zärtlicher Erinnerungen
tieftiefinneres Geläut
zu verachten, um des bangen jungen

Falken willen, dessen Blut und Sorgen
zu begreifen er sich nicht erließ.
Dafür war er auch wie mitgehoben,
wenn der Vogel, den die Herren loben,
glänzend von der Hand geworfen, oben
in dem mitgefühlten Frühlingsmorgen
wie ein Engel auf den Reiher stieß.

CORRIDA
IN MEMORIAM MONTEZ, 1830

Seit er, klein beinah, aus dem Toril
ausbrach, aufgescheuchten Augs und Ohrs,
und den Eigensinn des Picadors
und die Bänderhaken wie im Spiel

hinnahm, ist die stürmische Gestalt
angewachsen – sieh: zu welcher Masse,
aufgehäuft aus altem schwarzen Hasse,
und das Haupt zu einer Faust geballt,

234

Falconry

To be a king, you have to learn to meet
mysterious challenges and not to flinch.
Often his chancellor would find him, late,
up in his tower. There he would dictate
to the attentive scribe (who squatted, hunched

before him) his own bold treatise on the art
of falconry; and he himself would spend
nights in the lonely mews, content
to carry on his fist a half-wild bird,
gradually to train and gentle it.
From time to time he would reject a thought
or he might wave away some recollection
which seemed to ring a peal of bells within,
for anything unquiet must be suppressed
in case it should alarm the anxious falcon

whose every fear and whim he strove to read.
At last it was as if he too could fly.
When like a bolt of light it left his hand
he rose into the April morning shared
with the noble bird, ascended…soared…
till like an Angel tumbling from the sky
it stooped and struck and left the heron dead.

Corrida
In Memoriam Montez, 1830

First it seemed small as it burst from the pens
but the loud violence to its eyes and ears,
the cruel persistence of the picadors,
the irritation of the teasing ribbons,

have swollen it in size and swelled its rage:
and now it is the instrument of fate,
the archetypal enemy, in hate
the sullen head clenched up into a savage

235

nicht mehr spielend gegen irgendwen,
nein: die blutigen Nackenhaken hissend
hinter den gefällten Hörnern, wissend
und von Ewigkeit her gegen Den,

der in Gold und mauver Rosaseide
plötzlich umkehrt und, wie einen Schwarm
Bienen und als ob ers eben leide,
den Bestürzten unter seinem Arm

durchläßt, – während seine Blicke heiß
sich noch einmal heben, leichtgelenkt,
und als schlüge draußen jener Kreis
sich aus ihrem Glanz und Dunkel nieder
und aus jedem Schlagen seiner Lider,

ehe er gleichmütig, ungehässig,
an sich selbst gelehnt, gelassen, lässig
in die wiederhergerollte große
Woge über dem verlornen Stoße
seinen Degen beinah sanft versenkt.

DON JUANS KINDHEIT

In seiner Schlankheit war, schon fast entscheidend,
der Bogen, der an Frauen nicht zerbricht;
und manchmal, seine Stirne nicht mehr meidend,
ging eine Neigung durch sein Angesicht

zu einer die vorüberkam, zu einer
die ihm ein fremdes altes Bild verschloß:
er lächelte. Er war nicht mehr der Weiner,
der sich ins Dunkel trug und sich vergoß.

Und während ein ganz neues Selbstvertrauen
ihn öfter tröstete und fast verzog,
ertrug er ernst den ganzen Blick der Frauen,
der ihn bewunderte und ihn bewog.

fist. And now it knows this is no game
to play with anyone, for now it rears
the bloody banderillos and prepares
with bristling, lowered horns to charge at *him*

who stands there still, as if a little bored,
dressed in his suit-of-lights, in perfect calm
as if this swarm of bees must be endured...
but then turns suddenly and lifts an arm

and lets it pass. The dark eyes shine
as if all were projected by their light:
the bull-ring, everything that it contains,
conceived within their darkness; in their blaze
made real at each quick movement of his gaze.

Then without any animosity
as if quite casual, as if lazily,
he sights at the black crest at the next rush
of the oncoming beast, and with a push
to the bright blade he thrusts it out of sight.

Don Juan's Childhood

His slender body grew, became the bow
no female hands would find the strength to force.
Often a look of interest would flow
across his features, then it would pass

and settle on a face he saw: some woman
from a painting long ago whose strangeness
made him smile. He had outgrown
that darkness he had filled with childhood's tears

and felt at ease and now began to use
a self-assurance that reached just too far:
he gravely met the test of women's eyes
admiring him and setting him on fire.

DON JUANS AUSWAHL

Und der Engel trat ihn an: Bereite
dich mir ganz. Und da ist mein Gebot.
Denn daß einer jene überschreite,
die die Süßesten an ihrer Seite
bitter machen, tut mir not.
Zwar auch du kannst wenig besser lieben,
(unterbrich mich nicht: du irrst),
doch du glühest, und es steht geschrieben,
daß du viele führen wirst
zu der Einsamkeit, die diesen
tiefen Eingang hat. Laß ein
die, die ich dir zugewiesen,
daß sie wachsend Heloïsen
überstehn und überschrein.

SANKT GEORG

Und sie hatte ihn die ganze Nacht
angerufen, hingekniet, die schwache
wache Jungfrau: Siehe, dieser Drache,
und ich weiß es nicht, warum er wacht.

Und da brach er aus dem Morgengraun
auf dem Falben, strahlend Helm und Haubert,
und er sah sie, traurig und verzaubert
aus dem Knieen aufwärtsschaun

zu dem Glanze, der er war.
Und er sprengte glänzend längs der Länder
abwärts mit erhobnem Doppelhänder
in die offene Gefahr,

viel zu furchtbar, aber doch erfleht.
Und sie kniete knieender, die Hände
fester faltend, daß er sie bestände;
denn sie wußte nicht, daß Der besteht,

Don Juan's Choice

And when the Angel came he ordered him:
Submit to me – prepare now to obey
all my decrees. From you I shall require
a light so bright that brightest lights grow dim!
At love you are no better than the rest
(you may not argue with me. I know best)
nevertheless you have a kind of glow:
many women will be led by you
down the steep path which ends in loneliness.
Permit to enter there those whom I choose,
to ripen and endure like Heloïse,
to outlive and outcry the wilderness.

Saint George

All through the darkness, all through the night, she,
torn from her sleep, a pale helpless maiden,
kneels and calls out and prays for him vainly:
His eyes – they devour me! Help me – the Dragon!

Through the dawn mist the knight on his charger
bright in his burnished hauberk and helmet
sees her there, kneeling, mesmerised, wretched,
marvelling, gazing up at the splendour

of himself and his horse and the bright-shining armour
charging gallantly hither and yonder
the blade of his broadsword hacking the air –
closer and closer, tempting the danger

that he equally fears and desires.
Kneeling, her hands clasped tight in each other
she prays that the knight will prevail and will save her,
somehow forgetful, in her despairing,

den ihr Herz, ihr reines und bereites,
aus dem Licht des göttlichen Geleites
niederreißt. Zuseiten seines Streites
stand, wie Türme stehen, ihr Gebet.

DAME AUF EINEM BALKON

Plötzlich tritt sie, in den Wind gehüllt,
licht in Lichtes, wie herausgegriffen,
während jetzt die Stube wie geschliffen
hinter ihr die Türe füllt

dunkel wie der Grund einer Kamee,
die ein Schimmern durchläßt durch die Ränder;
und du meinst der Abend war nicht, ehe
sie heraustrat, um auf das Geländer

noch ein wenig von sich fortzulegen,
noch die Hände, – um ganz leicht zu sein:
wie dem Himmel von den Häuserreihn
hingereicht, von allem zu bewegen.

BEGEGNUNG IN DER KASTANIEN-ALLEE

Ihm ward des Eingangs grüne Dunkelheit
kühl wie ein Seidenmantel umgegeben
den er noch nahm und ordnete: als eben
am andern transparenten Ende, weit,

aus grüner Sonne, wie aus grünen Scheiben,
weiß eine enzelne Gestalt
aufleuchtete, um lange fern zu bleiben
und schließlich, von dem Lichterniedertreiben
bei jedem Schritte überwallt,

of the One who must always prevail –
with her, safeguarding her from all evil,
wrenched down from the Heavens by force of her prayer,
watching the battle, tall as a tower.

Lady on a Balcony

S heathed in cool wind she steps like someone drawn,
  bright in the brightness, out into the open;
leaving the image of the room behind,
fitting the doorway as if shaped and ground

and shining darkly like a cameo
at edges where a little light breaks through.
Surely the night has only now begun
now, as she comes to lay her hands upon

the coolness of the balcony's stone coping,
prepared to leave behind all heaviness;
offered to heaven, high above the houses,
to float there and to drift with everything.

Encounter in the Avenue of Chestnuts

T he cool green darkness on first entering
  was like a cloak of silk he drew around him,
and the translucent tunnel sent a gleam:
at that same moment, distantly approaching

under green sunshine, as through panes of green
and scarcely moving, still so far away,
a solitary white presence seemed to shine
under that drenching light, and finally,
its features clearer now, continued on:

ein helles Wechseln auf sich herzutragen,
das scheu im Blond nach hinten lief.
Aber auf einmal war der Schatten tief,
und nahe Augen lagen aufgeschlagen

in einem neuen deutlichen Gesicht,
das wie in einem Bildnis verweilte
in dem Moment, da man sich wieder teilte:
erst war es immer, und dann war es nicht.

DIE SCHWESTERN

Sieh, wie sie dieselben Möglichkeiten
anders an sich tragen und verstehn,
so als sähe man verschiedne Zeiten
durch zwei gleiche Zimmer gehn.

Jede meint die andere zu stützen,
während sie doch müde an ihr ruht;
und sie können nicht einander nützen,
denn sie legen Blut auf Blut,

wenn sie sich wie früher sanft berühren
und versuchen, die Allee entlang
sich geführt zu fühlen und zu führen:
Ach, sie haben nicht denselben Gang.

ÜBUNG AM KLAVIER

Der Sommer summt. Der Nachmittag macht müde;
sie atmete verwirrt ihr frisches Kleid
und legte in die triftige Etüde
die Ungeduld nach einer Wirklichkeit,

he watched a golden shimmer dance and leap
on it, retreating at each pace.
Then suddenly the shade grew still more deep
and eyes wide open looked out from a face

described in brilliant detail as it passed,
captured in time – fixed as in a picture
within the instant while they passed each other:
one moment there forever, then, quite lost.

The Sisters

How differently each one of them pursues
options that were for both of them the same;
it is as if exactly similar rooms
were occupied by different histories.

Each of them knows that she supports the other
although in weary fact she leans on her,
for to support lies quite outside their power:
blood remains blood but carries them no further,

and though their hands stay kind and they caress,
attempting as they stroll the promenade
to lead and at the same time to be led,
yet neither one can keep the other's pace.

Piano Practice

Breathing the fresh scent of her cotton dress,
feeling the summer buzzing drowsily,
she made a cut-and-dried *étude* express
how bored she was with unreality,

die kommen konnte: morgen, heute abend –,
die vielleicht da war, die man nur verbarg;
und vor den Fenstern, hoch und alles habend,
empfand sie plötzlich den verwöhnten Park.

Da brach sie ab; schaute hinaus, verschränkte
die Hände; wünschte sich ein langes Buch –
und schob auf einmal den Jasmingeruch
erzürnt zurück. Sie fand, daß er sie kränkte.

DIE LIEBENDE

Das ist mein Fenster. Eben
bin ich so sanft erwacht.
Ich dachte, ich würde schweben.
Bis wohin reicht mein Leben,
und wo beginnt die Nacht?

Ich könnte meinen, alles
wäre noch Ich ringsum;
durchsichtig wie eines Kristalles
Tiefe, verdunkelt, stumm.

Ich könnte auch noch die Sterne
fassen in mir; so groß
scheint mir mein Herz; so gerne
ließ es ihn wieder los

den ich vielleicht zu lieben,
vielleicht zu halten begann.
Fremd, wie niebeschrieben
sieht mich mein Schicksal an.

Was bin ich unter diese
Unendlichkeit gelegt,
duftend wie eine Wiese,
hin und her bewegt,

hungry for something real: later today –
or else tomorrow – or already here
but still concealed? Tall and proprietary,
the windows held the pampered park for her.

She broke off, clasped her hands and gazed outside.
The smell of jasmine hanging in the air
was sickening. She gestured it away.
She wished she had a good long book to read.

The Woman in Love

A waking softly, I
can see my window's panes.
I seem to float away –
How much of this is mine?
Where does the Night begin?

I might believe that all
were mine – all this around me,
transparent as a crystal's
darkness, and as profoundly

still. I feel I might
encompass all the stars –
the human heart is great
and mine would even loose

him I begin to love,
perhaps hold prisoner –
and what will destiny prove,
illegible, obscure?

How do I come to rest
in this infinity
of meadow-fragrances,
moved so contrarily –

rufend zugleich und bange,
daß einer den Ruf vernimmt,
und zum Untergange
in einem Andern bestimmt.

DAS ROSEN-INNERE

Wo ist zu diesem Innen
    ein Außen? Aug welches Weh
legt man solches Linnen?
Welche Himmel spiegeln sich drinnen
in dem Binnensee
dieser offenen Rosen,
dieser sorglosen, sieh:
wie sie lose im Losen
liegen, als könnte nie
eine zitternde Hand sie verschütten.
Sie können sich selber kaum
halten; viele ließen
sich überfüllen und fließen
über von Innenraum
in die Tage, die immer
voller und voller sich schließen,
bis der ganze Sommer ein Zimmer
wird, ein Zimmer in einem Traum.

DAMEN-BILDNIS AUS DEN
ACHTZIGER-JAHREN

Wartend stand sie an den schwergerafften
    dunklen Atlasdraperien,
die ein Aufwand falscher Leidenschaften
über ihr zu ballen schien;

beseeching, yet in fear
that one will hear my prayer –
destined to disappear
submerged within another?

The Heart of the Rose

Where is the outwardness
      to what lies here, within?
Whose wound was ever dressed,
bandaged in such fine linen?
Reflected here, what skies
lie open and at ease
as in a lake within
these open roses
in which all softly rests
as if no accidental hand
could shake or make it spill?
Unable to contain
the riches that are theirs
they pour out the excess
sharing their inwardness
to enrich the days; until
the whole of summer seems
one great room, a room within a dream.

Portrait of a Lady of the Eighteen-Eighties

She stands waiting, where the heavy curtains
    with their densely-pleated satin seem
to overpower her with a sombre presence
and to flaunt a meretricious drama:

seit den noch so nahen Mädchenjahren
wie mit einer anderen vertauscht:
müde unter den getürmten Haaren,
in den Rüschen-Roben unerfahren
und von allen Falten wie belauscht

bei dem Heimweh und dem schwachen Planen,
wie das Leben weiter werden soll:
anders, wirklicher, wie in Romanen,
hingerissen und verhängnisvoll, –

daß man etwas erst in die Schatullen
legen dürfte, um sich im Geruch
von Erinnerungen einzulullen;
daß man endlich in dem Tagebuch

einen Anfang fände, der nicht schon
unterm Schreiben sinnlos wird und Lüge,
und ein Blatt von einer Rose trüge
in dem schweren leeren Medaillon,

welches liegt auf jedem Atemzug.
Daß man einmal durch das Fenster winkte;
diese schlanke Hand, die neuberingte,
hätte dran für Monate genug.

DAME VOR DEM SPIEGEL

Wie in einem Schlaftrunk Spezerein
löst sie leise in dem flüssigklaren
Spiegel ihr ermüdetes Gebaren;
und sie tut ihr Lächeln ganz hinein.

Und sie wartet, daß die Flüssigkeit
davon steigt; dann gießt sie ihre Haare
in den Spiegel und, die wunderbare
Schulter hebend aus dem Abendkleid,

she feels like a stranger – someone else
stands remembering those years of girlhood
her face weary under piled-up tresses,
virginal in spite of ruche-trimmed dresses,
knowing they betray her – all those folds

listening to her, spying on her sadness,
overhearing plans she half-intends
for a life as people live in stories,
fateful, passionate and rich in portents:

to lay away within her treasury
something precious and forever guard it;
daydream in its scent and memory;
knowing this at last is real, to write it

in her journal: is there now a voice
which the writing does not turn to falsehood?
Will she take one petal of a rose
to keep it in the heavy hollow locket

rhythmically rising, falling with her breathing?
If her slender hand with its new rings
were once to wave in greeting through the window –
would she feel this was enough, for now?

Lady at her Mirror

Fatigued, she lets her features gradually
dissolve in the clear glass, as one might sift
the spices added to a sleeping-draught.
She steeps her smile in it, then lets it dry.

She waits a little. Loosening her hair
she watches as it pours into the glass
and sees revealed above her evening-dress,
perfect and pale, the shoulders shining there.

trinkt sie still aus ihrem Bild. Sie trinkt,
was ein Liebender im Taumel tränke,
prüfend, voller Mißtraun; und sie winkt

erst der Zofe, wenn sie auf dem Grunde
ihres Spiegels Lichter findet, Schränke
und das Trübe einer späten Stunde.

DIE GREISIN

Weiße Freundinnen mitten im Heute
lachen und horchen und planen für morgen;
abseits erwägen gelassene Leute
langsam ihre besonderen Sorgen,

das Warum und das Wann und das Wie,
und man hört sie sagen: Ich glaube –;
aber in ihrer Spitzenhaube
ist sie sicher, als wüßte sie,

daß sie sich irren, diese und alle.
Und das Kinn, im Niederfalle,
lehnt sich an die weiße Koralle,
die den Schal zur Stirne stimmt.

Einmal aber, bei einem Gelache,
holt sie aus springenden Lidern zwei wache
Blicke und zeigt diese harte Sache,
wie man aus einem geheimen Fache
schöne ererbte Steine nimmt.

Alone, she silently drinks in her picture
doubtfully tasting something that a lover
would thirstily, would frenziedly devour,

then calls her maid to tidy up what lies
untidily upon the mirror's floor:
the lights; the furniture; the darkening hours.

The Old Woman

Friends in white dresses, absorbed in today,
chatter, laugh and propose their tomorrows.
Meanwhile others, a little away,
quietly ponder problems or sorrows:

their whys and their whens and the hows,
murmuring *perhaps* or *I wonder*. Under
her starched lace cap she knows what she knows –
knows they have found no true answers

sees how they all are mistaken
and lets her white head fall
forward again, till the chin
meets the white coral clasp of her shawl

and once, as the laughter continues,
discloses her undeceived eyes –
just as one might lift out
from their own secret cabinet
family jewels, dazzling and obdurate.

DAS BETT

Laß sie meinen, daß sich in privater
Wehmut löst, was einer dort bestritt.
Nirgend sonst als da ist ein Theater;
reiß den hohen Vorhang fort –: da tritt

vor den Chor der Nächte, der begann
ein unendlich breites Lied zu sagen,
jene Stunde auf, bei der sie lagen,
und zerreißt ihr Kleid und klagt sich an,

um der andern, um der Stunde willen,
die sich wehrt und wälzt im Hintergrunde;
denn sie konnte sie mit sich nicht stillen.
Aber da sie zu der fremden Stunde

sich gebeugt: da war auf ihr,
was sie am Geliebten einst gefunden,
nur so drohend und so groß verbunden
und entzogen wie in einem Tier.

DER FREMDE

Ohne Sorgfalt, was die Nächsten dächten,
die er müde nicht mehr fragen hieß,
ging er wieder fort; verlor, verließ –.
Denn er hing an solchen Reisenächten

anders als an jeder Liebesnacht.
Wunderbare hatte er durchwacht,
die mit starken Sternen überzogen
enge Fernen auseinanderbogen
und sich wandelten wie eine Schlacht;

The Bed

Let them believe that solitude and woe
will melt away what we engage in here.
No other place is such a theatre:
draw up the curtain and the stage will show

before the Chorus of the Night who sing
their own interminable song, the Hour
of the Lovers, by whose grace they cling,
tearing her garments – on account of her

who stands and waits behind her on the stage
where, apprehensively, she twists and turns,
whom nothing in her power can quieten.
She bends towards this other Hour, so strange

and unfamiliar, finding her possessed
of what she long ago found in her lover;
although more menacing, of greater power –
committed and withdrawn as in a beast.

The Stranger

Paying no heed to friends or family,
again he went – impatiently – away.
Some things were left, some lost. The journeying
by night, so dear to him, was quite distinct –

unlike the nights of love. He used to watch
nights wondrously overlaid and stitched
with brilliant stars – they seemed to force
apart, to bend the distances;
they wavered as a battle ebbs and flows.

andre, die mit in den Mond gestreuten
Dörfern, wie mit hingehaltnen Beuten,
sich ergaben, oder durch geschonte
Parke graue Edelsitze zeigten,
die er gerne in dem hingeneigten
Haupte einen Augenblick bewohnte,
tiefer wissend, daß man nirgends bleibt;
und schon sah er bei dem nächsten Biegen
wieder Wege, Brücken, Länder liegen
bis an Städte, die man übertreibt.

Und dies alles immer unbegehrend
hinzulassen, schien ihm mehr als seines
Lebens Lust, Besitz und Ruhm.
Doch auf fremden Plätzen war ihm eines
täglich ausgetretnen Brunnensteines
Mulde manchmal wie ein Eigentum.

DIE ANFAHRT

War in des Wagens Wendung dieser Schwung?
   War er im Blick, mit dem man die barocken
Engelfiguren, die bei blauen Glocken
im Felde standen voll Erinnerung,

annahm und hielt und wieder ließ, bevor
der Schloßpark schließend um die Fahrt sich drängte,
an die er streifte, die er überhängte
und plötzlich freigab: denn da war das Tor,

das nun, als hätte es sie angerufen,
die lange Front zu einer Schwenkung zwang,
nach der sie stand. Aufglänzend ging ein Gleiten

die Glastür abwärts; und ein Windhund drang
aus ihrem Aufgehn, seine nahen Seiten
heruntertragend von den flachen Stufen.

Then there were other nights in which the moon-
bright villages, like thieves, surrendered
and gave up their loot; some nights displayed
an old stone mansion guarding its demesne
(his head would turn to look and he would dream
just for an instant, this might be his home;
knowing there is nowhere we can remain).
The road would curve again and let him see
bridges and open fields and bridleways
extending to the hyperbolic towns.

To have the strength to leave such things behind
was more to him than life itself could mean,
meant more than prowess, more than what he owned.
But sometimes somewhere in a foreign land
the humble, hollowed, daily-trodden stone
beside an ancient well could signify
a whole domain; a landed property.

The Arrival

What stirred one so – the motion of the vehicle
taking the bend? Or suddenly to see
baroque angels in a field of bluebells –
once more as real as in the memory?

Their image came and went, then parkland
running beside the drive and pacing it,
then falling back – for we had reached the gate
which seemed to give an order, a command

at which, obediently complying,
the long façade swung by. At last we stopped.
The glazed door caught the sun and flashed its eyes,

in front of it a greyhound swiftly rose
avoiding, narrowly, its opening,
and slipped his leanness down the shallow steps.

DIE SONNENUHR

Selten reicht ein Schauer feuchter Fäule
aus dem Gartenschatten, wo einander
Tropfen fallen hören und ein Wander-
vogel lautet, zu der Säule,
die in Majoran und Koriander
steht und Sommerstunden zeigt;

nur sobald die Dame (der ein Diener
nachfolgt) in dem hellen Florentiner
über ihren Rand sich neigt,
wird sie schattig und verschweigt –.

Oder wenn ein sommerlicher Regen
aufkommt aus dem wogenden Bewegen
hoher Kronen, hat sie eine Pause;
denn sie weiß die Zeit nicht auszudrücken,
die dann in den Frucht- und Blumenstücken
plötzlich glüht im weißen Gartenhause.

SCHLAF-MOHN

Abseits im Garten blüht der böse Schlaf,
in welchem die, die heimlich eingedrungen,
die Liebe fanden junger Spiegelungen,
die willig waren, offen und konkav,

und Träume, die mit aufgeregten Masken
auftraten, riesiger durch die Kothurne –:
das alles stockt in diesen oben flasken
weichlichen Stengeln, die die Samenurne

(nachdem sie lang, die Knospe abwärts tragend,
zu welken meinten) festverschlossen heben:
gefranste Kelche auseinanderschlagend,
die fieberhaft das Mohngefäß umgeben.

The Sundial

S cent of decay sometimes, from damp shade
  where the water-drops hear one another
falling and a migrant bird
calls and calls, to the column, set there
in the coriander and the marjoram,
counting hours of summer time –

but the lady passing with her servant,
in her bright straw hat, halts and pauses
by it; drowns it in her shadow,
shields it so that it falls silent;

and when summer rain begins to fall
and a wind blows up and makes the high
tree-tops tremble – how could any sundial
find a way to count the ripened hours
glowing in the painted fruits and flowers
pictured on the white pavilion's walls?

Opium Poppy

F ar from the other flowers, sinful sleep
  grows here: any who softly enter in
are free to taste the love of young reflections,
accommodating, open, not too deep:

they may see dreams appear in antic masks,
raised up as tall as giants upon buskins:
such gifts are stored within these supple stems
which bear the seed-heads, still supporting them
erect and sealed, though they had seemed prepared
to fade, had let tired buds hang down:
now they make valanced petals open wide
around their capsules, each a fevered sun.

DIE FLAMINGOS
JARDIN DES PLANTES, PARIS

In Spiegelbildern wie von Fragonard
ist doch von ihrem Weiß und ihrer Röte
nicht mehr gegeben, als dir einer böte,
wenn er von seiner Freundin sagt: sie war

noch sanft von Schlaf. Denn steigen sie ins Grüne
und stehn, auf rosa Stielen leicht gedreht,
beisammen, blühend, wie in einem Beet,
verführen sie verführender als Phryne

sich selber; bis sie ihres Auges Bleiche
hinhalsend bergen in der eignen Weiche,
in welcher Schwarz und Fruchtrot sich versteckt.

Auf einmal kreischt ein Neid durch die Volière;
sie aber haben sich erstaunt gestreckt
und schreiten einzeln ins Imaginäre.

PERSISCHES HELIOTROP

Es könnte sein, daß dir der Rose Lob
zu laut erscheint für deine Freundin: Nimm
das schön gestickte Kraut und überstimm
mit dringend flüsterndem Heliotrop

den Bülbül, der an ihren Lieblingsplätzen
sie schreiend preist und sie nicht kennt.
Denn sieh: wie süße Worte nachts in Sätzen
beisammenstehn ganz dicht, durch nichts getrennt,
aus der Vokale wachem Violett
hindüftend durch das stille Himmelbett –:

so schließen sich vor dem gesteppten Laube
deutliche Sterne zu der seidnen Traube
und mischen, daß sie fast davon verschwimmt...
die Stille mit Vanille und mit Zimmt.

The Flamingos
Jardin des Plantes, Paris

Looking-glass images by Fragonard
could no more paint their white, capture their red,
than if one boasting of his mistress said:
She was still full of sleep...she was so soft...

Upon pink stems, like flowers in a bed,
together among the plants, all slightly turned,
enchanting, irresistible as Phryne,
self-enchanted, they will shyly hide

their white-rimmed eyes deep in their downy sides
among soft, secret colours; blacks and reds.
A jealous screech shrills through the aviary:
they spread their wings and stretch out necks, surprised.
And each alone stalks silently away
on slender legs, out into fantasy.

Persian Heliotrope

It may be that the beauty of the rose
seems much too flagrant, that it seems too loud
to celebrate and sing your mistress' praise:
this flower's embroidered subtlety exceeds

the bulbul's love-song singing in her bowers
to serenade her though it does not know her.
Like words by night in whispered messages,
urgent and dense, no silences between,
a violet whispering of voices sends
its fragrance to perfume the attentive heavens

and, lucent stars affixed to silken berries,
the blossom shines against its latticed leaves
breathing a sweet intoxicating potion:
silence spiced with vanilla, cinnamon.

SCHLAFLIED

Einmal wenn ich dich verlier,
wirst du schlafen können, ohne
daß ich wie eine Lindenkrone
mich verflüstre über dir?

Ohne daß ich hier wache und
Worte, beinah wie Augenlieder,
auf deine Brüste, auf deine Glieder
niederlege, auf deinen Mund.

Ohne daß ich dich verschließ
und dich allein mit Deinem lasse
wie einen Garten mit einer Masse
von Melissen und Stern-Anis.

DER PAVILLON

Aber selbst noch durch die Flügeltüren
mit dem grünen regentrüben Glas
ist ein Spiegeln lächelnder Allüren
und ein Glanz von jenem Glück zu spüren,
das sich dort, wohin sie nicht mehr führen,
einst verbarg, verklärte und vergaß.

Aber selbst noch in den Stein-Guirlanden
über der nicht mehr berührten Tür
ist ein Hang zur Heimlichkeit vorhanden
und ein stilles Mitgefühl dafür –,

und sie schauern manchmal, wie gespiegelt,
wenn ein Wind sie schattig überlief;
auch das Wappen, wie auf einem Brief
viel zu glücklich, überstürzt gesiegelt,

Lullaby

If one day I have to lose you
what could bring you sleep – unless
like a lime-tree's restless branches
I still whisper on above you?

Unless I keep watch about you
while you sleep – speak words which seem
to caress your breasts, your limbs,
fall like eyelids on your mouth.

Unless I enclose you safely
with all that you truly own –
as if in a quiet garden
stocked with balm and star-anise.

The Pavilion

Even today behind these folding doors
and even through the rain-dimmed greenish glass
in silent spaces standing bare and closed,
traces remain of smiling courtesies –
fortune lay hidden, blazed, and then was lost.

Even today around the carved stone garlands
above this doorway, now no longer used,
the habit of a secrecy remains
and old complicities survive and brood:

they seem to tremble sometimes, like reflections
when air disturbs still water-surfaces.
Like a seal on a letter, the escutcheon
(sealed hastily in dangerous happiness)

redet noch. Wie wenig man verscheuchte:
alles weiß noch, weint noch, tut noch weh –.
Und im Fortgehn durch die tränenfeuchte
abgelegene Allee

fühlt man lang noch auf dem Rand des Dachs
jene Urnen stehen, kalt, zerspalten:
doch entschlossen, noch zusammzuhalten
um die Asche alter Achs.

DIE ENTFÜHRUNG

Oft war sie als Kind ihren Dienerinnen
entwichen, um die Nacht und den Wind
(weil sie drinnen so anders sind)
draußen zu sehn an ihrem Beginnen;
doch keine Sturmnacht hatte gewiß
den riesigen Park so in Stücke gerissen,
wie ihn jetzt ihr Gewissen zerriß,
da er sie nahm von der seidenen Leiter
und sie weitertrug, weiter, weiter…:

bis der Wagen alles war.

Und sie roch ihn, den schwarzen Wagen,
um den verhalten das Jagen stand
und die Gefahr.
Und sie fand ihn mit Kaltem ausgeschlagen;
und das Schwarze und Kalte war auch in ihr.
Sie kroch in ihren Mantelkragen
und befühlte ihr Haar, als bliebe es hier,
und hörte fremd einen Fremden sagen:
Ichbinbeidir.

still stands, still speaks. How little, after all,
was driven away: here everything remembers,
weeps and hurts. Your footsteps fall
on the neglected pathway, damp with tears,

by which you leave, and you will not forget
the cracked urns standing on the parapet
frosted and crazed, continuing to hold
the ashes of the cries no longer heard.

The Abduction

Often in childhood she had escaped from
watchful servants in order to feel
(only outdoors did it seem real)
in their own element night and the storm.
From the ladder of silk he takes her
(hearing the voice of her conscience speak,
for no storm-wind ever ravaged the park
to cause such havoc as this night's work)
she is lifted – carried off further, further,

to the coach: the coach is all that is there.

The threat of pursuit, a feeling of danger
in the chill coach with its musty odour.
Feeling the darkness, feeling the moisture
sinking into the cold within,
she hides her face in the greatcoat collar,
touches her hair (it was all she could bring)
and for no good reason the lips of a stranger
whisper to her:
I-am-with-you-I-am-here.

ROSA HORTENSIE

Wer nahm das Rosa an? Wer wußte auch,
       daß es sich sammelte in diesen Dolden?
Wie Dinge unter Gold, die sich entgolden,
entröten sie sich sanft, wie im Gebrauch.

Daß sie für solches Rosa nichts verlangen.
Bleibt es für sie und lächelt aus der Luft?
Sind Engel da, es zärtlich zu empfangen,
wenn es vergeht, großmütig wie ein Duft?

Oder vielleicht auch geben sie es preis,
damit es nie erführe vom Verblühn.
Doch unter diesem Rosa hat ein Grün
gehorcht, das jetzt verwelkt und alles weiß.

DAS WAPPEN

Wie ein Spiegel, der, von ferne tragend,
       lautlos in sich aufnahm, ist der Schild;
offen einstens, dann zusammenschlagend
über einem Spiegelbild

jener Wesen, die in des Geschlechts
Weiten wohnen, nicht mehr zu bestreiten,
seiner Dinge, seiner Wirklichkeiten
(rechte links und linke rechts),

die er eingesteht und sagt und zeigt.
Drauf, mit Ruhm und Dunkel ausgeschlagen,
ruht der Spangenhelm, verkürzt,

den das Flügelkleinod übersteigt,
während seine Decke, wie mit Klagen,
reich und aufgeregt herniederstürzt.

Pink Hydrangea

Who could have guessed this pink? And who could know
that it would gather here within these clusters? –
Their colour gradually fades away,
as gold on gilded things wears out through use.

There is no charge. No payment is required.
Does pink endure to smile down from on high?
Shall there be Angels, welcoming and tender,
when, prodigal as scent, it has to die?

But maybe they will simply let it fall,
perhaps to spare it from its withering.
Beneath the pink a green, forever listening
and withering already, now knows all.

The Coat-of-Arms

Like a distant looking-glass that chooses
its reflections, gathering them in,
the escutcheon, open once, forecloses
on its symbols – picturing the clansmen

dwelling in the region, peaceably
settled in hereditary estates,
undisputed now: showing property
and lineage, right placed left and left placed right;

vouching for them, stating and proclaiming.
Fixed above the shield, foreshortened, brutal,
stippled by the shadows, dark with chivalry,

stands the helmet with its crest and wings
looking as if challenged to a battle:
visor lowered, armed, provoked and ready.

DER JUNGGESELLE

Lampe auf den verlassenen Papieren,
und ringsum Nacht bis weit hinein ins Holz
der Schränke. Und er konnte sich verlieren
an sein Geschlecht, das nun mit ihm zerschmolz;
ihm schien, je mehr er las, er hätte ihren,
sie aber hatten alle seinen Stolz.

Hochmütig steiften sich die leeren Stühle
die Wand entlang, und lauter Selbstgefühle
machten sich schläfernd in den Möbeln breit;
von oben goß sich Nacht auf die Pendüle,
und zitternd rann aus ihrer goldnen Mühle,
ganz fein gemahlen, seine Zeit.

Er nahm sie nicht. Um fiebernd unter jenen,
als zöge er die Laken ihrer Leiber,
andere Zeiten wegzuzerrn.
Bis er ins Flüstern kam; (was war ihm fern?)
Er lobte einen dieser Briefeschreiber,
als sei der Brief an ihn: Wie du mich kennst;
und klopfte lustig auf die Seitenlehnen.
Der Spiegel aber, innen unbegrenzter,
ließ leise einen Vorhang aus, ein Fenster –:
denn dorten stand, fast fertig, das Gespenst.

DER EINSAME

Nein: ein Turm soll sein aus meinem Herzen
und ich selbst an seinen Rand gestellt:
wo sonst nichts mehr ist, noch einmal Schmerzen
und Unsäglichkeit, noch einmal Welt.

Noch ein Ding allein im Übergroßen,
welches dunkel wird und wieder licht,
noch ein letztes, sehnendes Gesicht
in das Nie-zu-Stillende verstoßen,

The Bachelor

Family papers underneath the lamplight;
    night soaks into the wooden cabinets.
Sometimes he lost himself in ancestry
though ancestors decayed as fast as he,
believing in the end their pride was his.
But he possessed no pride that was not theirs.

In its own wooden pride each empty chair
stands stiffly by the wall, while self-esteem
is comfortable on softer furniture.
The night rains down into the pendulum,
a golden mill set there to grind and pour
a fine unsteady stream: his time.

Excitedly he rummages and studies
as if he robbed the dead of history,
as if to strip the sheets from naked bodies:
nothing was secret, nothing alien! Whispering
to himself, enthusing over a letter
as if he thought himself the one addressed –
How well you understand! I'm quite impressed! –
delighted, beats the arm-rest of his chair.
The mirror over-rides its inhibitions
disposes of a window and some curtains
and shows the ghost, now almost ready there.

The Solitary

No! I refuse! My heart shall be a tower
    and I must set myself upon its edge
and in that nothingness must be once more
all world, all pain, all that cannot be said.

A solitary thing, still lost in huge excess
time after time darkening and lightening –
the last surviving image of all yearning,
cast out into infinite restlessness.

267

noch ein äußerstes Gesicht aus Stein,
willig seinen inneren Gewichten,
das die Weiten, die es still vernichten,
zwingen, immer seliger zu sein.

DER LESER

Wer kennt ihn, diesen, welcher sein Gesicht
wegsenkte aus dem Sein zu einem zweiten,
das nur das schnelle Wenden voller Seiten
manchmal gewaltsam unterbricht?

Selbst seine Mutter wäre nicht gewiß,
ob *er* es ist, der da mit seinem Schatten
Getränktes liest. Und wir, die Stunden hatten,
was wissen wir, wieviel ihm hinschwand, bis

er mühsam aufsah: alles auf sich hebend,
was unten in dem Buche sich verhielt,
mit Augen, welche, statt zu nehmen, gebend
anstießen an die fertig-volle Welt:
wie stille Kinder, die allein gespielt,
auf einmal das Vorhandene erfahren;
doch seine Züge, die geordnet waren,
blieben für immer umgestellt.

DER APFELGARTEN
BORGEBY-GÅRD

Komm gleich nach dem Sonnenuntergange,
sieh das Abendgrün des Rasengrunds;
ist es nicht, als hätten wir es lange
angesammelt und erspart in uns,

268

And still this final, ultimate stone face,
consenting to endure its heaviness –
while silently the distances destroy
what they compel to ever greater joy.

The Reader

Who knows this stranger who has turned his face
away from life to live another life –
which nothing interrupts except the swift
and forceful turning of each printed page?

Even a mother might not recognise
her son, lost in the world that lies below him,
steeped in his own shadow. What can we know –
who live our lives so governed by mere hours –

of other lives he may have lived and lost
before he looks up, heavy now and burdened
with all the matter which his book contains?
As children rise from play and look around
his eyes now turn to all that lies outside,
towards the world again made manifest;
but yet his face, for all its discipline,
will never while he lives change back again.

The Apple Orchard
Borgeby gård

Come when the sun has set and you shall see
the green of evening stain the grassy ground:
how easily we might believe that we
ourselves had tended it and sown,

um es jetzt aus Fühlen und Erinnern,
neuer Hoffnung, halbvergeßnem Freun,
noch vermischt mit Dunkel aus dem Innern,
in Gedanken vor uns hinzustreun

unter Bäume wie von Dürer, die
das Gewicht von hundert Arbeitstagen
in den überfüllten Früchten tragen,
dienend, voll Geduld, versuchend, wie

das, was alle Maße übersteigt,
noch zu heben ist und hinzugeben,
wenn man willig, durch ein langes Leben
nur das Eine will und wächst und schweigt.

DIE BERUFUNG

Da aber als in sein Versteck der Hohe,
sofort Erkennbare: der Engel, trat,
aufrecht, der lautere und lichterlohe:
da tat er allen Anspruch ab und bat

bleiben zu dürfen der von seinen Reisen
innen verwirrte Kaufmann, der er war;
er hatte nie gelesen – und nun gar
ein *solches* Wort, zu viel für einen Weisen.

Der Engel aber, herrisch, wies und wies
ihm, was geschrieben stand auf seinem Blatte,
und gab nicht nach und wollte wieder: *Lies.*

Da las er: so, daß sich der Engel bog.
Und war schon einer, der gelesen *hatte*
und konnte und gehorchte und vollzog.

so that in present feeling and remembering
of new-born hopes, of half-forgotten joys
seasoned with darker feelings deep within,
we could believe we now spread out before us

the heavy harvest of a hundred days
beneath old trees that Dürer might have drawn
which stand there silent, serving, seeking ways
to bear the fruits which weigh their branches down;

to raise and proffer what grows, measureless,
for those who long and patiently endure –
who all their lives sustaining their desire
for one thing only, silently increase.

The Summons

He knew at once the lofty, shining One
who came to him and entered his retreat,
so upright and so blazing with white light,
yet he entreated to be left alone:

He was a simple merchant, he was tired,
was just returned weary in every limb,
such matters were for wise men not for him,
he was unlettered, he did not aspire...

The lordly Angel persevered and pressed
him: *He must read the sacred text*
and still insisted and still urged him: *Read!*

At last he read – and then the Angel bowed.
Now it was read, was learned, and he was taught.
He was the one who acted and who wrought.

DER BERG

Sechsunddreißig Mal und hundert Mal
hat der Maler jenen Berg geschrieben,
weggerissen, wieder hingetrieben
(sechsunddreißig Mal und hundert Mal)

zu dem unbegreiflichen Vulkane,
selig, voll Versuchung, ohne Rat, –
während der mit Umriß Angetane
seiner Herrlichkeit nicht Einhalt tat:

tausendmal aus allen Tagen tauchend,
Nächte ohne gleichen von sich ab
fallen lassend, alle wie zu knapp;
jedes Bild im Augenblick verbrauchend,
von Gestalt gesteigert zu Gestalt,
teilnahmslos und weit und ohne Meinung –,
um auf einmal wissend, wie Erscheinung,
sich zu heben hinter jedem Spalt.

DER BALL

Du Runder, der das Warme aus zwei Händen
im Fliegen, oben, fortgiebt, sorglos wie
sein Eigenes; was in den Gegenständen
nicht bleiben kann, zu unbeschwert für sie,

zu wenig Ding und doch noch Ding genug,
um nicht aus allem draußen Aufgereihten
unsichtbar plötzlich in uns einzugleiten:
das glitt in dich, du zwischen Fall und Flug

noch Unentschlossener: der, wenn er steigt,
als hätte er ihn mit hinaufgehoben,
den Wurf entführt und freiläßt –, und sich neigt
und einhält und den Spielenden von oben
auf einmal eine neue Stelle zeigt,
sie ordnend wie zu einer Tanzfigur,

The Mountain

Thirty-six times, then a hundred times,
      conjuring the mountain to his page,
driven back to it then dragged away
thirty-six times then a hundred times,

he turns to the volcano yet again
joyful, mesmerised, yet unsuccessful,
trying like a madman in his line
to capture the unrepresentable...

Judging them imperfect, insufficient,
it lets nights unequalled slip away
reappearing on a thousand days
to exploit each image in its moment;
letting each manifestation grow,
generous, impartial, unconcerned,
knowing at once as though by revelation
how to show its face at every window.

The Ball

Roundness! so high, so prodigal in losing
      warmth of our hands that was not yours to spill!
What cannot live in objects – too ethereal,
too little *thing*, though just enough a thing
drawn from the rank-and-file of otherness
silently, suddenly, to enter into us –
has entered into you; who stay unsure
whether to fall or fly, but as you rise
catch up the throw itself to set it free
and lift it with you high into the air;
then you come dipping down to earth as though
to show the players something, somewhere new,
arranging them as if it were a dance:

um dann, erwartet und erwünscht von allen,
rasch, einfach, kunstlos, ganz Natur,
dem Becher hoher Hände zuzufallen.

DAS KIND

Unwillkürlich sehn sie seinem Spiel
lange zu; zuweilen tritt das runde
seiende Gesicht aus dem Profil,
klar und ganz wie eine volle Stunde

welche anhebt und zu Ende schlägt.
Doch die Andern zählen nicht die Schläge,
trüb von Mühsal und vom Leben träge;
und sie merken gar nicht, wie es trägt –,

wie es alles trägt, auch dann, noch immer,
wenn es müde in dem kleinen Kleid
neben ihnen wie im Wartezimmer
sitzt und warten will auf seine Zeit.

DER HUND

Da oben wird das Bild von einer Welt
aus Blicken immerfort erneut und gilt.
Nur manchmal, heimlich, kommt ein Ding und stellt
sich neben ihn, wenn er durch dieses Bild

sich drängt, ganz unten, anders, wie er ist;
nicht ausgestoßen und nicht eingereiht,
und wie im Zweifel seine Wirklichkeit
weggebend an das Bild, das er vergißt,

um dennoch immer wieder sein Gesicht
hineinzuhalten, fast mit einem Flehen,
beinah begreifend, nah am Einverstehen
und doch verzichtend: denn er wäre nicht.

until, awaited, coveted by all,
swift, simple, artless, wholly natural,
you fall to meet the cupped high-reaching hands.

The Child

Absent-mindedly they watch its play:
looking on for hours they sometimes see
the rounded childish face, so present, briefly
turn from profile – facing them directly

like a little clock that's set to chime,
striking all its hours, falling silent.
Preoccupied with their own cares and lives
they neither count its hours nor know its time

nor do they see the heaviness it carries,
silent beside them as in some waiting-room
when, weary now, still in its little dress
it sits and waits for its own time to come.

The Dog

A world of image is what counts – up there –
and is continually renewed by sight.
Yet sometimes some *thing* secretly comes near,
stays by him as he seeks to penetrate

beyond the image – like himself, apart,
inferior and, fundamentally,
though not excluded yet kept separate.
Unsure, he gives the image his reality

and then, forgetting, none the less
holds up his face to it beseechingly
and, nearly satisfied, nearly accepts
but still rejects it – for he could not *be*.

DER KÄFERSTEIN

Sind nicht Sterne fast in deiner Nähe
und was giebt es, das du nicht umspannst,
da du dieser harten Skarabäe
Karneolkern gar nicht fassen kannst

ohne jenen Raum, der ihre Schilder
niederhält, auf deinem ganzen Blut
mitzutragen; niemals war er milder,
näher, hingegebener. Er ruht

seit Jahrtausenden auf diesen Käfern,
wo ihn keiner braucht und unterbricht;
und die Käfer schließen sich und schläfern
unter seinem wiegenden Gewicht.

BUDDHA IN DER GLORIE

Mitte aller Mitten, Kern der Kerne,
Mandel, die sich einschließt und versüßt, –
dieses Alles bis an alle Sterne
ist dein Fruchtfleisch: Sei gegrüßt.

Sieh, du fühlst, wie nichts mehr an dir hängt;
im Unendlichen ist deine Schale,
und dort steht der starke Saft und drängt.
Und von außen hilft ihm ein Gestrahle,

denn ganz oben werden deine Sonnen
voll und glühend umgedreht.
Doch in dir ist schon begonnen,
was die Sonnen übersteht.

The Scarab

S urely the stars are not so far distant
  and there is little you do not possess
each time you take the scarab in your hand;
whose hard, cornelian heart encompasses

the *space* which presses down and firms its scales
and, never more accessible or gentler,
enters the blood, accompanies and fills.
Forever near them, for millennia

never made use of and left undisturbed
it hangs above the scarabs as they rest,
dreaming, locked up inside themselves, secure,
and rocking in the cradle of its heaviness.

Buddha in Glory

C entre of centres, heart within all hearts,
  sweet inmost kernel, self-enclosed, within
itself growing more sweet – to you whose fruit
is all of this, reaching the stars: Greetings.

Now you can know that nothing more depends
on you, your shell set in infinity
where energy from outside radiance
augments the potent juices flowing through;

high above your fiery suns are turned
within their courses – all is turned around
while silently within yourself is born
what will exceed and will outlast all suns.

Notes

22 *Früher Apollo* and *Archaischer Torso Apollos*, the initial poems of Parts I and II of the *Neue Gedichte*, give a sample of the differences in mood and technique between the two parts.

22 *Mädchen-Klage*. It has been suggested that the three poems, *Mädchen-Klage, Früher Apollo*, and *Liebes-Lied* are a trilogy illustrating themes of puberty, adolescence, and adult love.

24 *Eranna an Sappho*. Eranna or Erinna was a young poet who lived on the Dorian island of Telos. According to the legend she died, aged nineteen, of a disappointed love for Sappho. It is now thought that they were not contemporary.

26 *Sappho an Alkaïos*. In his letter of 25 July 1907 to his wife Clara, Rilke writes: 'Alkaïos was a poet who stands [painted] on an antique vase in front of Sappho, his lyre in hand and with downcast head, and one knows that he has said to her – "Weaver of darkness, pure one, Sappho with your smile as sweet as honey, words press to my lips but shame restrains me..." And she replies – "If there were the desire in you for noble and elevated things, if the words upon your tongue were not unworthy, then you would not have lowered your gaze in shame and you would have spoken, as is right."' (Mytilene is the capital city of Lesbos, where Sappho was born and where she lived until, for reasons not known, she went to live in exile in Sicily.) A number of letters around this date discuss the choices of art against life, artistic mastery against sexual or romantic love: *dieser Gott* is certainly in this case Apollo and not Eros.

28 *Grabmal eines jungen Mädchens*. The image of Death in this poem may be taken literally, or else may be seen as figuring the loss of virginity; symbolising the death of childhood and of its integrity.

28 *Opfer*. The 'sacrifice', as in the preceding poem, may represent the sacrifice of childish innocence; the price which must be paid for growing into sexual maturity and the capacity for adult love.

30 *Östliches Taglied*. 'Aubade', 'Dawn-song', as against 'Serenade', 'Evening-song'. The chanciness, sadness and fleetingness of sexual love also darken the tones of the next poem, *Abisag*.

32 *Abisag*. 1 Kings 1: 1-4.

34 *David singt vor Saul*. 1 Samuel: 'And Saul's servants said to him, "Behold now, an evil spirit from God is tormenting you. Let our lord now command your servants, who are before you, to seek out a man who is skilful in playing the lyre; and when the evil spirit

from God is upon you, he will play it, and you will be well"...And David came to Saul and entered his service. And Saul loved him greatly...And whenever the evil spirit from God was upon Saul, David took the lyre and played it with his hand, so Saul was refreshed, and all was well, and the evil spirit departed from him.'

36 *Josuas Landtag*. Joshua 6:24.

40 *Der Auszug des verlorenen Sohnes*. Luke 15. Rilke was certainly also familiar with the Rodin sculpture of a kneeling, leaning, male figure, *L'Enfant Prodigue*.

40 *Der Ölbaum-Garten*. Rilke has humanised and secularised Christ's monologue in the garden of Gethsemane in a manner likely to cause offence to some Christians. Nevertheless the poem can be read both as religious and as anti-religious: both interpretations seem credible.

42 *Pietà*. Rilke has taken the theme of the mourning of Christ but has turned it into love-poetry: it is the elegy of Mary Magdalene for her dead lover.

46 *Buddha* (Als ob er horchte). In a number of letters written in the summer and autumn of 1905, Rilke refers to a sculptured Buddha in the garden of Rodin's house at Meudon. At this time Rilke was still full of awe and admiration for Rodin himself. The poem perhaps most expresses the young artist's worship of Rodin and his veneration for the sculptor's magisterial integrity and powers.

48 *L'Ange du Méridien*. The figure is that of the angel with the sundial, on the southern side of the cathedral.

48 *Die Kathedrale*. It is held that this poem refers not to a particular cathedral but to cathedrals in general. The 'cathedral poems' of the *Neue Gedichte* also include the preceding poem, as well as *Das Portal*, *Die Fensterrose*, and *Das Kapitäl*.

50 *Das Portal*. The poem has been variously understood by various commentators. Possibly Rilke's intention in Part II is both reverent and ironic, for he is a master of double meanings.

A more literal translation of the end of Part III might read as follows:

> in which a world they do not see,
> a world of wildness still not trodden down,
> figures and animals, set there as if to harm them,
> contorts and trembles, holds them nonetheless –
>
> because those presences, like acrobats
> perform such wild, convulsive gesturing
> only so that the staff upon their forehead shall not fall.

54 *Die Fensterrose.* The 'lazy pacing of its paws' has been understood as an image for the succession of the cathedral columns, creating an hypnotic effect by their stillness and by their repetition.
58 *Der Gefangene.* A number of letters of the period (winter 1905 to spring of 1906) testify to Rilke's growing discomfort and sense of oppression in his work as Rodin's secretary. What had seemed to be his great good fortune now felt like imprisonment. The break came on 11 May 1906, and thereafter Rilke returned to Paris and took lodgings in the rue Cassette. The whole history of Rodin's declension from 'God' to 'gaoler' had taken less than six months.
60 *Der Panther* (Paris 1902 or 1903). Almost certainly the earliest of the poems of the *Neue Gedichte*. In a letter of 17 March 1926 (the final year of his life) Rilke writes that the poem came about as the result of Rodin's strenuous urging that he should 'work like a painter or sculptor, *from life*'.
62 *Die Gazelle* (Paris 1907). Rilke's letter to Clara of 13 June 1907 gives a prose account of his study of *Gazella Dorcas* at the Jardin des Plantes.
62 *Das Einhorn.* Not, in this instance, a study from life from the Jardin des Plantes, but from the famous tapestry in the Musée de Cluny, *La Dame à la Licorne.*
64 *Sankt Sebastian.* Probably the source is the Botticelli painting of the subject, in the Kaiser Friedrich Museum in Berlin.
64 *Der Stifter.* Portraits of the donors who commissioned religious pictures were often included in the paintings, sometimes as performers in the drama, sometimes as bystanders, sometimes self-evidently as 'the donors', as in the outer panels of the 'Holy Lamb' triptych by the van Eycks.
66 *Der Engel.* Rilke occasionally uses the imagery of sculpture and of the foundry for his purposes as a poet. Here, the sculptor-Angel has first wrought the 'you' apostrophised in the poem, then 'breaks you from your mould' like a figure cast in metal or in plaster.
68 *Römische Sarkophage.* Sarcophagus literally means 'flesh-eater'. The ancient Greeks believed that their stone coffins dissolved and absorbed the bodies interred in them.
72 *Die Spitze.* The poem is clearly an important statement of Rilke's faith in the absolute virtue of 'making'. A passage in *Malte Laurids Brigge* supports this reading, as does a letter of 16 August 1920.
76 *Die Erwachsene.* A striking pre-echo of this Rilke poem of 1907 can be found in Edvard Munch's picture *Puberty*, painted in 1895.
76 *Tanagra.* Rilke had seen in the Louvre a number of small terracotta sculptures from Tanagra. (Letter to Clara of 26 September 1902.)

82 *Todes-Erfahrung.* An *in memoriam* poem written for the Countess Luise Schwerin, who had died the previous year.

86 *Im Saal.* Both this and the preceding poem are believed to originate from a visit to the Château de Chantilly, described in Rilke's letter to Clara of 1 June 1906. The group of poems from *Im Saal* to *Die Treppe der Orangerie* share an 'historical' bias. Many of them return to the younger Rilke's romantic preoccupations with chivalry and with the gaining or losing of honour.

86 *Letzter Abend.* Frau Nonna is Julie, Freifrau von Nordeck zur Rabenau, whose first husband had been killed at the battle of Königgrätz in 1866.

88 *Jugend-Bildnis meines Vaters.* Josef Rilke was for ten years a cadet in the artillery, but was in the end prevented by ill health from gaining his commission. Instead, he made his living as a railway-official and, finally, as an inspector of railways.

90 *Der König.* It is now thought that the subject is taken from a painting in the Hamburger Kunsthalle: *Edward VI Signing a Death Warrant*, by John Pettie (1839-93).

96 *Der Marmor-Karren* (June 1907). The great Rodin sculpture, *Le Penseur*, was installed in April 1906: the poem may have been inspired by the sculpture's transportation to its site in front of the Panthéon.

100 *Das Karussell.* The poem contains, in addition to its human subject matter, a faithful description of the merry-go-round which still stands in the playground of the Luxembourg Gardens.

102 *Spanische Tänzerin* (Letter to Clara of 26 April 1906).

102 *Der Turm.* The first part of the poem moves laboriously and is complex: images of 'ascent' and 'descent', 'rising' and 'falling', 'mountain' and 'abyss' change place with one another. The puzzling *'behangen wie ein Stier'* is possibly Rilke's image for the great bells suspended from the roof-timbers of the tower. Immediately following this image the poem opens out and the scene becomes fluent and pastoral. Joachim de Patenier (1475-1524): Netherlandish painter whose pictures often showed simultaneously, side by side, events that belonged to different times.

104 *Der Platz.* A letter to Karl van der Heydt, dated 31 July 1906, further describes Rilke's impressions of this scene: the Flemish painter David Teniers (1610-90) is invoked to conjure up the bustling, sweltering confusion and richness of the annual fair in the market-place of Furnes. The equestrian statue is that of Charles the Bold, ambitious ruler of an almost independent Burgundian duchy.

108 *Béguinage.* Lambert Bègue, priest of Liège in the 12th century, founded the order and gave it his name. The Béguines are a lay order, not bound by strict vows, whose members are free to leave the community and to marry.

110 *Die Marien-Prozession.* In a letter to Clara of 2 February 1907, Rilke discusses his choice of the adjective 'chryselephantine'.

116 *Hetären-Gräber.* This poem exists in an earlier prose-poem version, as do also the poems *Geburt der Venus* and *Orpheus. Eurydike. Hermes.* (See below.)

118 *Orpheus. Eurydike. Hermes.* The poem is probably connected with a bas-relief of the subject seen by Rilke, whether in Naples, in the Louvre, or in Rome.

124 *Alkestis.* In the version by Euripides, Admetus has offended the goddess Artemis and she sentences him to die. He is reprieved only because his wife, Alcestis, is willing to die in his stead and to take his place in the Underworld. Later, Hercules comes to visit the mourning Admetus, whose hospitality he repays by himself descending to the Underworld. There he wrestles with Death and defeats him. Alcestis is brought back to life and she is restored to Admetus.

130 *Geburt der Venus.* The prime source of the poem is the painting by Botticelli. The Italian goddess Venus became identified with the Greek Aphrodite, who first came to land either at Paphos or at Cythera (according to different legends). She is the goddess, above all, of generation and of sexuality, but also, appropriately, of gambling and of all games of chance. It has been suggested that the brutal image of the last stanza, the dead, gutted dolphin, represents the afterbirth.

134 *Die Rosenschale.* Roses were always of the greatest significance to Rilke, and are frequently his symbol for the wondrous, the extreme, the transcendent. This poem is related to *Das Roseninnere* and to various other Rilke poems, but perhaps especially to Rilke's own mysterious epitaph:

> *Rose, oh reiner Widerspruch, Lust*
> *Niemands Schlaf zu sein unter soviel*
> *Lidern.*

142 *Archaïscher Torso Apollos.* This important poem is more minatory and more complex than the straightforwardly lyrical *Früher Apollo* of Part I.

142 *Kretische Artemis.* Artemis is the goddess of woods and forests and of the chase. She is a moon-goddess and especially a goddess of

women. Herself virgin, she is the helper and benefactress of women in childbirth.

144 *Leda.* W.B. Yeats's great set-piece, also a sonnet ('A sudden blow: the great wings beating still...'), was written in 1923. It bears some resemblance to Rilke's poem written in 1907 or 1908.

144 *Delphine.* In classical legend, dolphins were friends and companions to sailors and often saved them from death by drowning. The Tritons were mermen, the sons and attendants of Poseidon and Amphitrite. In Ovid's *Metamorphoses*, the disguised Bacchus revenges himself on the sailors who had planned to sell him into slavery: their ship is immobilised with ropes of ivy and the seamen are gradually transformed into dolphins.

146 *Die Insel der Sirenen.* In a letter to Clara of 18 February 1907, Rilke describes his sight of the golden islands in the Gulf of Salerno, and he recalls the story of Odysseus, lashed for his own protection to the mast of his ship.

The sequence of poems from *Die Insel der Sirenen* up to and including *Römische Campagna* seem related in mood, all of them stark, menacing, ironical or simply sad. They concern themselves in general with images of violence, ruination or misfortune. In all of them there seems to be an element of fear. The pessimism is sometimes ameliorated at the end of the poem, as in *Der Auferstandene, Irre im Garten,* or in *Der Blinde.*

148 *Klage um Antinous.* The mourning voice can only be that of the Emperor Hadrian. However it was the Emperor himself who was responsible for the deification of the dead youth, and in consequence for 'hurling him as far as the stars'.

150 *Klage um Jonathan.* 2 Samuel 1.

150 *Tröstung des Elia.* 1 Kings.

152 *Saul unter den Propheten.* 1 Samuel.

154 *Samuels Erscheinung vor Saul.* 1 Samuel 28.

156 *Ein Prophet.* Ezekiel 5-8.

160 *Absoloms Abfall.* 2 Samuel 15-19.

162 *Esther.* Esther 5: 1-2. On the advice of his counsellors, King Ahasuerus deposed his rebellious Queen. To replace her he chose and married the beautiful Esther to whom he became devoted. Later, Esther, a Jewess, was able to save the Jews of Persia from persecution by Haman, the King's corrupt chief minister.

164 *Der aussätzige Konig.* 2 Chronicles 26:16-21. King Uzziah of Judah disputed with his priests and was punished by being immediately struck with leprosy.

166 *Legende von den drei Lebendigen und den drei Toten.* The subject

matter is probably taken from frescoes seen by Rilke in Pisa, during his stay in Viareggio in 1903.

166 *Der König von Münster.* Jan Bockelson, also known as John of Leyden, Anabaptist and polygamist. In 1535, Münster was taken by the Catholics and the disgraced Bockelson was tried and put to death.

168 *Toten-Tanz.* Rilke's poem is related to Baudelaire's *Danse Macabre* from the group *Tableaux parisiens* in *Les Fleurs du Mal.*

170 *Das Jüngste Gericht.* There is an important, much more discursive poem of the same title in the earlier collection, *Das Buch der Bilder.*

170 *Die Versuchung.* A painting by Hieronymus Bosch, *The Temptation of St Anthony,* may have been a source for this poem.

174 *Der Reliquienschrein.* An uncollected poem, *Der Goldschmied,* was begun by Rilke on the same day as this poem and shares some of its subject matter.

174 *Das Gold.* Meröe in Ethiopia, city of the kings of Kush, was famous for its gold and also for its iron-workings.

176 *Der Stylit.* In his letter to Clara of 19 October 1907, Rilke identifies Baudelaire's *Une Charogne (Les Fleurs du Mal)* and Flaubert's *La Legende de St-Julien-l'hospitalier* as works critically important in the development of 'the kind of objective statement we believe we recognise in Cézanne'.

178 *Die Ägyptische Maria.* St Mary of Egypt, a reformed harlot, lived the life of a hermit in the desert where she finally died. She was buried by the monk Zosimus, aided by a lion.

180 *Der Auferstandene.* Rilke's doctrine of unpossessive love (or perhaps, more baldly, of 'unpossession') is amongst his most frequently recurring themes.

182 *Magnificat.* Luke 1:39-56.

184 *Eva.* In his letter to Clara of 31 August 1902, Rilke mentions the figures of Adam and Eve on the façade of the cathedral of Notre Dame.

186 *Irre im Garten.* The Chartreuse de Champmol, visited by Rilke on his return journey from Viareggio in April 1903.

188 *Aus dem Leben eines Heiligen.* The subject is St Francis of Assisi.

192 *Eine von den Alten.* The Rilke poem is related to Baudelaire's *Les petites Vieilles,* from *Tableaux parisiens* in *Les Fleurs du Mal.*

198 *Die Gruppe* (Letter to Dora Heydrich of 14 July 1907). The figures are those of the 'Père Rollin' group of performers, who are the subject of the Fifth of the *Duino Elegies* and were almost certainly Picasso's models for *Les Saltimbanques.*

202 *Schwarze Katze.* Montaigne: *'Quand je me joue à ma chatte, qui sait si elle passe son temps de moi, plusque je ne fais d'elle?'*

202 *Vor-Ostern*. The title means literally 'pre-Easter' (Easter Eve).

206 *Auswanderer-Schiff*. The last lines bear some similarity to the final image of *Geburt der Venus*.

210 *Römische Campagna*. The Terme di Caracalla are the last important edifice on the Via Appia as it leads out of Rome and into the Campagna to the south-east.

212 *Pappageien-Park*. '*die Ara*': large, spectacularly-coloured genus of parrots and macaws.

214 *Die Parke*. It is thought that the poem draws on Rilke's experience of Versailles, Chantilly and various estate-parks in Europe, and perhaps on images of parkland in paintings by Van Gogh with which Rilke was familiar.

222 *Bildnis*. The subject is Eleanora Duse. Various letters from November 1906 and a much later letter to the Princess Marie of Thurn und Taxis Hohenlohe, dated 12 July 1912, testify to Rilke's glowing admiration for the actress.

226 *Spätherbst in Venedig*. During the year 1907 Rilke devoted time to the study of Venetian history. The 'General des Meeres' is Admiral Carlo Zeno.

228 *Ein Doge*. Signory: 'Governing body of medieval Italian republic' (OED). In Venice this was the 'Council of Ten' by whom the decisions of the Doge could be ratified or constrained.

228 *Die Laute*. The lutanist is Tullia d'Aragona, a famous 16th-century courtesan, poetess and musician.

234 *Falken-Beize*. The Emperor Frederick the Great (1194-1240) was the author of a substantial work on the art of falconry: *De arte venandi cum avibus*.

234 *Corrida*. Rilke explains the 'galear del Toro' to his wife in a letter of 8 September 1907. At the time he had not yet seen a bullfight.

238 *Don Juans Auswahl*. Rilke makes the Angel's instructions to Don Juan serve as propaganda for the doctrine of 'love without possession'.

238 *Sankt Georg*. Two prefatory pieces exist, of only slightly earlier date (August 1907): *Skizze zu einem Sankt Georg*, and *Du aber Alles erwartende einsame Reine*.

244 *Die Liebende*. The nature and scope of the 'self', the destiny of women, their capacity for abnegation of that 'self' in sexual love, are Rilke's subjects here as elsewhere.

246 *Damen-Bildnis aus den Achtziger-Jahren*. The letter to Clara of 7 June 1907 describes an exhibition of paintings in the little Château de Bagatelle in the Bois de Boulogne: portraits of women from the years 1870 to 1900. Rilke praises especially a portrait by Manet.

248 *Dame vor dem Spiegel.* Mirrors and mirror-images, reality and reflection, Narcissism, and 'life' as compared with the images of 'art', are touched on in this as in the preceding poem.

252 *Das Bett.* The personified 'Hours' of the poem are the 'Hour of Love' and the 'Hour of Parting'. (Or perhaps 'The Pleasures of Love' and 'The Pains of Love'.) Here is yet another piece in praise of abnegation.

252 *Der Fremde.* Rilke evidently valued this poem as a homily addressed to himself. He quotes from it in his letter of 21 October 1913 to Lou Andreas-Salomé, as a lesson he should never have allowed himself to forget.

258 *Die Flamingos* (1907 or 1908). The relationship between this poem, *Der Panther* and *Die Gazelle* comes from more than their location in the Jardin des Plantes. Phryne: 4th-century Greek courtesan of legendary beauty.

258 *Persiches Heliotrop. Bülbül*: Asian song-thrush.

260 *Der Pavillon.* Rilke's letter to Clara of 2 December 1905 describes a visit to Versailles with Rodin which may have prompted this poem.

264 *Rosa Hortensie.* The companion-poem to the *Blaue Hortensie* of Part I, showing a considerable shift in mood from the earlier poem.

266 *Der Einsame.* The pervasively stony lines of the poem, comfortless but for its last line, are in marked contrast to the mood of the immediately preceding *Der Junggeselle*, with its sharp images, its irony and its gleeful malice: its *Schadenfreude*. The two poems are dated '2 August 1908', and 'before mid-August 1908'.

268 *Der Leser.* A similar poem, *Der Lesende*, is to be found in the *Buch der Bilder*. Written in 1901, it has the poet's own voice speaking as 'the reader'.

270 *Die Berufung.* In the later editions of the *Neue Gedichte* the title has been changed to *Mohammeds Berufung*.

272 *Der Berg.* Hokusai made two collections of drawings of Mount Fuji: the *Thirty-Six Views of Fuji*, and the later *One Hundred Views of Fuji*.

272 *Der Ball.* The poems, *Der Apfelgarten, Die Berufung, Der Berg,* and *Der Ball* all share the theme of 'vocation'.

274 *Das Kind.* The verb 'anheben' applies to a clock in the preparatory setting of its striking-mechanism; before it actually strikes.

Index of English Titles

289

Index of German Titles